"*The Positivity Workbook for Teens* provides a treasure trove of activities for teens to learn about who they are at their best! This book shows teens how to use their strengths to thrive in the good times, navigate the bad times, and work on areas they want to improve. It is practical, relatable, doable, and, most importantly, it's uplifting. The teen years are fraught with self-doubt and stress—this book offers an antidote. I highly recommend it for all teachers, parents, and teens."

>—**Lea Waters, PhD**, leading global figure in strengths and parenting, psychology researcher at the University of Melbourne, and author of *The Strength Switch*

"*The Positivity Workbook for Teens* is a timely guide through the best of positive psychology. This book teaches essential skills in building resilience, and increasing happiness and well-being. By learning to know and use their character strengths, teens embark on a journey of self-development and personal growth. This workbook is an excellent resource for anyone working with teens to teach them positive skills to protect and build their well-being."

>—**Carmel Proctor, PhD**, psychologist and psychotherapist, director of the Positive Psychology Research Centre (PPRC), and coauthor of *Strengths Gym*

"This book is packed with an abundance of powerful, research-backed tools to help teens take immediate action to improve their resilience, relationships, and their joy in life. I'll be recommending this to the parents and teens that I work with!"

>—**Rachelle Plummer, PsyD**, child psychologist at Cincinnati Children's Hospital Medical Center

"With its focus on the particular challenges of teens, this workbook addresses a glaring gap in the positive psychology literature. The examples are highly compelling and timely, the writing style is engaging and accessible, and the many hands-on activities will foster insight and empower teens to create their own happiness."

> —**Jaime Kurtz, PhD**, professor of psychology at James Madison University, and author of *The Happy Traveler*

"Chapter by chapter—with inspiring quotations, pithy explanations, and practical exercises—Goali Saedi Bocci and Ryan Niemiec outline what young people can do to live life to the fullest. As a researcher, an educator, and a father of teenage boys, the far-reaching benefits of this book were immediately evident to me. It brims with the artfulness and experience required to make positive psychology exciting and accessible for young people."

> —**Roger Bretherton, PsyD**, associate professor of psychology at the University of Lincoln, UK

"We all know that happiness can be learned. However, it is not learned in one go; some work is certainly required. *The Positivity Workbook for Teens* invites teens to invest in their greatest treasure—themselves—by working through many user-friendly and engaging activities. A real gem!"

> —**Ilona Boniwell, PhD**, CEO of Positran; professor; MAPP strategic program leader at Anglia Ruskin University; and author of seven books and many tangible tools, including *Strengths Cards*

the positivity workbook for teens

skills to help you increase optimism, resilience & a growth mindset

GOALI SAEDI BOCCI, PhD
RYAN M. NIEMIEC, PsyD

Instant Help Books
An Imprint of New Harbinger Publications, Inc.

Publisher's Note

This publication is designed to provide accurate and authoritative information in regard to the subject matter covered. It is sold with the understanding that the publisher is not engaged in rendering psychological, financial, legal, or other professional services. If expert assistance or counseling is needed, the services of a competent professional should be sought.

Distributed in Canada by Raincoast Books

Copyright © 2020 by Goali Saedi Bocci and Ryan M. Niemiec
New Harbinger Publications, Inc.
5674 Shattuck Avenue
Oakland, CA 94609
www.newharbinger.com

Cover design by Amy Shoup

Acquired by Wendy Millstine

Edited by Brady Kahn

Library of Congress Cataloging-in-Publication Data on file

Printed in the United States of America

22   21   20

10   9   8   7   6   5   4   3   2   1   First Printing

For

All the teens and their families who have opened up their hearts and allowed me the great privilege of bearing witness to this incredible phase in their lives. You have taught me far more than I could have ever imagined.

—Goali

For

The Rooster

With gratitude for helping me stay strong through my teenage years and beyond,

Your best bud,

—Ryan

acknowledgments

We are grateful for the researchers in the fields of positive psychology and character strengths as well as those researchers and practitioners who have bravely pioneered new territory to help teens discover well-being, use their character strengths, and build greater resilience. Special appreciation goes to the following practitioners who offered us sound advice and suggestions surrounding the most effective research-backed strategies they use with teens: Carmel Proctor, Rebecca Park, Roger Bretherton, Mark Liston, Masaya Okamoto, Lynn Ochs, Marissa Rowley, and Tijuana Evans. Thank you!

We are also grateful for the editors and staff at New Harbinger who believe in and have supported this book from the outset and helped champion it to what you have in your hands now.

Goali would also like to thank her mentors and advisors along the way, too many to list, but most notably Drs. Jennifer Wisdom, Don Pope-Davis, and Claytie Davis III for their infinite collective wisdom and unending support. She would also like to thank her tirelessly supportive husband, Bret, for so enthusiastically encouraging this incredible journey into an entirely new field. Much gratitude also goes to Dr. Ryan Niemiec for sharing in this collaboration and for his unparalleled insight, zest, and kindness in helping her dip her toes into such unchartered territory. Finally, she would like to thank her parents for raising her with endless stacks of books.

Ryan would also like to thank his VIA colleagues, Breta Cooper, Neal Mayerson, Kelly Aluise, Chris Jenkins, Ruth Pearce, Donna Mayerson, Clare Blankemeyer, and Jeff Seibert, and his loving wife, Rachelle, mother Sue, father Joe, brother Joey, and sisters Lisa and Monica for their ongoing support and belief in the best parts of him. And, of course, gratitude to his future teenagers—a long, long time away!—Rhys, Ryland, and Maya, whom he promises to lovingly support through their trials and tribulations.

Finally, we are grateful to you for taking the first step and picking up this book to improve your well-being or the well-being of someone you care for. We are honored to have the opportunity to offer these tools to you.

Contents

Part 4: Cultivating What Matters Most
Meaning → Well-Being

Part 5: Your Goals, Your Life
Accomplishment → Well-Being

Part 6: Healthy Body, Healthy Mind
Your Positive Health → Well-Being

letter to parents and professionals

Happiness is not something ready made. It comes from your own actions.

—His Holiness the Dalai Lama

Who doesn't want to be happier? Whether it's an image of a group of smiling faces from a favorite TV show or pictures of friends plastered all over social media, we all know what sheer excitement, contentment, and bliss can look like. And yet sometimes happiness can seem so far away. Or worse, it can feel fake or inauthentic when you are just pretending that you're having a blast like everyone else.

Too many times, teens come into therapy and say they used to be bubbly and excited and that their enthusiasm has faded away due to stressors of life. Other times, they delight in being a "realist" and believe the pursuit of happiness is a futile one, refusing the help of anyone who tries to lift their mood and spirits. Sound familiar? Wherever teens may fall on this continuum, the field of positive psychology has over the last couple of decades provided a plethora of research findings that can help them get back to their most radiant self.

When asked, most teens can immediately remember a time in the past when they were content, living each day to the fullest without a tremendous number of worries. When they describe those times, they say they were living life authentically, without pretense, and with no concerns about pleasing parents or friends. They were simply free to be the best version of themselves. The aim of this workbook is to help them return to that place—a place where they can flourish and find fulfillment.

While getting to "happy" can certainly be an admirable goal, it can also provide the challenge of a moving target. What made us happy yesterday may no longer make us happy today, and frankly, many times we can be wrong about what we think will make us happy. Further, if we focus on only ourselves, we may realize we are never as fulfilled as we might be when giving back to others and connecting as a member of a larger community. Therefore, the purpose of many activities in this workbook is to educate and inspire teens to take concrete steps toward greater well-being for both their own and the collective good.

By learning to identify their signature strengths, teens will start familiarizing themselves with a healthy sprinkling of their own attributes that can empower them through the ups and downs of life. This book has adapted a well-being framework called PERMA™, developed by the founder of positive psychology, Dr. Martin Seligman, to challenge teens to focus on ways they can use their own character strengths to cultivate positive emotions (part 1), bolster their engagement in life (part 2), enhance positive and healthy relationships (part 3), imbue meaning (part 4), increase accomplishments (part 5), and improve their physical health (part 6).

As they do this, they will gain a toolkit equipped with the best concepts from positive psychology with a special focus on well-being. Positive psychology exercises are a great fit for teens because they tend to be brief, easy to understand and apply, focused on amplifying the good, and based in research showing they can make a positive impact. These activities can help with common teen situations, from enhancing motivation (activity 8) to battling boredom (activity 13) to dealing with bullies (activity 14) and managing FOMO (activity 26). Beyond problem solving and crisis management, other activities in this book aim to increase teens' overall sense of meaning in life, as they learn to savor experiences (activity 20), cultivate gratitude (activity 21), practice mindfulness (activity 22), and experience profound moments of awe and inspiration (activity 24).

While there is no required order for completing the activities in this workbook, getting a sampling of each part can be helpful for setting up teens for success. Starting with the signature strengths survey in the introduction would be helpful. From there, teens might opt to start with the activities and parts of the book that appeal most to them and then branch out to areas where they could use a boost. There are also supplementary materials available for download at the website for this book: http://www.newharbinger.com/46028. (See the very back of this book for more details.)

Whether you are a parent, therapist, counselor, or coach, be assured that the activities in this book come from a place of hope and zest for all that the teenage years can be. While bumps in the road are certainly to be expected, learning to meet these challenges is an integral skill that will set up teens to navigate the peaks and valleys ahead.

With gratitude, we are excited for you to embark upon this journey! Thank you for letting us be a small part of this precious time in your teen's life.

Goali Saedi Bocci, PhD

Ryan M. Niemiec, PsyD

introduction

What lies behind you and what lies in front of you, pales in comparison to what lies inside of you.

—Ralph Waldo Emerson

The teen years are filled with periods of tremendous excitement as well as great challenges—peaks of joy, laughter, and pleasure alongside valleys of anguish, isolation, and confusion. Some of it you'll remember; some you'll soon forget. Whether it's the first time you hold your driver's license in hand, go to the prom, or get accepted into college, it is a decade of new experiences. Crushes and breakups, getting hired or turned down, making the school play or getting rejected from the varsity team, it's all part of the flow of the teen years. Emotional roller coasters are part of these experiences, as you try to navigate the turbulence and gain some sense of traction and a feeling of being grounded in your life. It can be easy for you to lose perspective and get lost in the negative, forgetting that you are a person with many inherent good qualities and tools you can use to build the positive and manage the roller coaster. This is where positive psychology comes in!

Formally established in 1998, positive psychology came about when researchers realized that too much attention to life challenges—such as depression, anxiety, trauma, and addictions—had been leaving out a critical piece of the puzzle. What makes life worth living? What about meaning and purpose and the pursuit of happiness? What about the millions of people who are not clinically diagnosed with a problem but could use a reminder of their strengths and a boost of courage, perseverance, and hope? Psychology and similar fields had been imbalanced because they were too focused on the negatives. It was time to bring science to what is best in human beings and to use those discoveries to help people overcome emotional barriers and build stronger relationships, use their strengths to become more resilient, and look at stress in a new way.

your well-being

It's easy to think about what you're not doing well. You can get lost in a worry about what someone at work or school said to you, upset that no one is responding to your Facebook or Instagram post, or think that you have no future when you look at your most recent grades report. We'll teach you not to ignore the negative or the reality of your stressors but to merge these with your strengths and other areas of your well-being.

A leading theory in positive psychology is called PERMA™, which stands for the five main areas of well-being that all human beings experience: P for positive emotions, E for engagement, R for relationships, M for meaning, and A for accomplishment. Here is a description and example of each area.

The PERMA™ model is the organizing framework for this book. It was developed by the founder of positive psychology, Martin Seligman, PhD, who graciously supported our use of it for this book. Like many researchers and practitioners, we've added a sixth pivotal area of well-being—health—making our book's structure PERMA-H.

Area of Well-Being	Description	Example
Positive emotions	Pleasurable feelings such as joy, excitement, interest, and peace	Donna felt a wave of joy from the positive comment her new Facebook friend made about the pictures she shared.
Engagement	Absorbing yourself in the task at hand	Neal was fully engaged in Snapchat as he and his brother shared videos and pictures of what they were doing in different cities.
Relationships (positive)	Creating and connecting in healthy relationships that enrich your life	Clare feels very connected to her boyfriend. They spend a lot of time together, especially on weekends, cooking, dancing, and watching Netflix together.
Meaning	Pursuing or experiencing a sense of connection and purpose that goes beyond yourself (with another person, an institution, or the larger universe)	Ruth experiences a deep sense of meaning when she takes nature photographs that fill her with awe and then shares them with her followers on Instagram.
Accomplishment	Reaching your goals; finding success through benchmarks, awards, or achievements in one or more domains of your life	Kelly worked very hard on her entrance exams, essays, and applications and was accepted into her choice of three universities.
Health	The experience of physical health and wellness that feels good in your body and mind. Health is more than simply the absence of disease; it is a feeling of vitality regardless of whether or not you are disease-free.	Breta has generally good health habits, as she eats and sleeps well, but feels especially vital and alive when she is active, playing softball, or attending a yoga class with friends.

your character strengths

Now for the most important part. You already possess the ingredients to make up your well-being! These ingredients are called *character strengths.* Researchers have discovered there are twenty-four character strengths that make up the positive part of your personality (your core identity). These are strengths like gratitude, bravery, teamwork, kindness, curiosity, fairness, hope, and creativity. Your character strengths are your personal pathways to greater meaning, positive emotions, relationships, and other areas of well-being and wellness you care about.

What You Need to Know About Your Character Strengths

1. You have all twenty-four of these qualities within you. Nobody has all twenty-four strengths perfectly developed or uses them all the time, but they are all there, waiting for you to focus on and develop. You might think of these strengths as seeds of potential in you.

2. Your highest strengths are referred to as your *signature strengths.* These are unique to you, just like your signature on a piece of paper. Your signature strengths likely come natural to you, are personally energizing, and best capture the real you.

3. You can develop or improve your use of any of your character strengths. For example, you can become more grateful, braver, funnier, or more hopeful.

4. Each strength can help you in its own way. For example, perseverance is probably going to help you a lot in getting through a difficult school subject, self-regulation is likely a critical strength for improving your health, while kindness and humor will probably help you develop more friendships.

5. Your character strengths can help you manage your stress and problems. Certainly, you can amplify the good in yourself and in your life with these strengths, but they are also key to overcoming adversity and getting through difficult life moments.

Now that you're beginning to learn about the importance of these qualities, it's time to discover your own signature strengths! To assess your strengths, we invite you to take the signature strengths survey below (adapted from the VIA Institute on Character). It's a quick test that will help you understand which character strengths might be your best sources of energy and connection.

Signature Strengths Survey

Read the following descriptions of the twenty-four character strengths that make up the positive part of your personality. Put a check in the box next to those strengths that you believe are absolutely essential to you, that define who you are as a person or are essential to who you are. For example, someone who has devoted his life to helping others might choose kindness as one of his essential strengths, someone who prides herself on being able to figure out other people might consider social intelligence key to who she is, and someone who is constantly seeking out new information might consider love of learning to be essential to him. Now review the boxes you checked, and choose the five strengths that best describe the person you are—and not the person you wish you could be. Circle those five strengths. Be sure to think about your life in general rather than how you've behaved in only one or two situations.

Essential to You	Character Strengths
	1. Creativity: You view yourself as a creative person; you see, do, and/or create things that are of use; you think of unique ways to solve problems and be productive.
	2. Curiosity: You are an explorer; you seek novelty; you are interested in new activities, ideas, and people; you are open to new experiences.
	3. Judgment/critical thinking: You are analytical; you examine things from all sides; you do not jump to conclusions but instead attempt to weigh all the evidence when making decisions.
	4. Love of learning: You often find ways to deepen your knowledge and experiences; you regularly look for.new opportunities to learn; you are passionate about building knowledge.
	5. Perspective: You take the "big picture" view of things; others turn to you for wise advice; you help others make sense of the world; you learn from your mistakes.
	6. Bravery: You face your fears and overcome challenges and adversity; you stand up for what is right; you do not shrink in the face of pain or inner tension or turmoil.
	7. Perseverance: You keep going and going when you have a goal in mind; you attempt to overcome all obstacles; you finish what you start.

Essential to You	Character Strengths
	8. Honesty: You are a person of high integrity and authenticity; you tell the truth even when it hurts; you present yourself to others in a sincere way; you take responsibility for your actions.
	9. Zest: You are enthusiastic toward life; you are highly energetic and activated; you use your energy to the fullest degree.
	10. Love: You are warm and genuine to others; you not only share but are open to receiving love from others; you value growing close and intimate with others.
	11. Kindness: You do good things for people; you help and care for others; you are generous and giving; you are compassionate.
	12. Social intelligence: You pay close attention to social nuances and the emotions of others; you have good insight into what makes people "tick"; you seem to know what to say and do in any social situation.
	13. Teamwork: You are a collaborative and participative member on groups and teams; you are loyal to your group; you feel a strong sense of duty to your group; you always do your share.
	14. Fairness: You believe strongly in an equal and just opportunity for all; you don't let personal feelings bias your decisions about others; you treat people the way you want to be treated.
	15. Leadership: You positively influence those you lead; you prefer to lead than to follow; you are very good at organizing and taking charge for the collective benefit of the group.
	16. Forgiveness: You readily let go of hurt after you are wronged; you give people a second chance; you are not vengeful or resentful; you accept people's shortcomings.
	17. Humility: You let your accomplishments speak for themselves; you see your own goodness but prefer to focus attention on others; you do not see yourself as more special than others; you admit your imperfections.
	18. Prudence: You are wisely cautious; you plan ahead and are conscientious; you are careful to not take undue risks or do things you might later regret.
	19. Self-regulation: You are a very disciplined person; you keep your bad habits from getting out of control; you stay calm and cool under pressure; you manage your impulses and emotions.

Essential to You	Character Strengths
	20. Appreciation of beauty and excellence: You notice the beauty and excellence around you; you are often awestruck by beauty, greatness, or the moral goodness you witness; you are often filled with wonder.
	21. Gratitude: You regularly experience and express thankfulness; you don't take the good things that happen in your life for granted; you tend to feel blessed in many circumstances.
	22. Hope: You are optimistic, expecting the best to happen; you believe in and work toward a positive future; you can think of many pathways to reach your goals.
	23. Humor: You are playful; you love to make people smile and laugh; your sense of humor helps you connect closely to others; you brighten gloomy situations with fun and jokes.
	24. Spirituality: Your life is infused with a sense of meaning and purpose; you feel a connection with something larger than yourself; your faith informs who you are and your place in the universe; you maintain a regular spiritual or religious practice.

Write your top five signature strengths below:

_____

_____

_____

_____

_____

Be sure to mark this page with your initial responses to the signature strengths survey and its definitions of the twenty-four character strengths. You'll want to refer back to it later. As you learn more about signature strengths in this book and home in on your own strengths, you might want to add to or subtract from your initial selection. This list is not set in stone.

taking action...ready, set, go!

Review the five signature strengths you highlighted in the survey. Take your signature strengths to the next level by memorizing them. Then try out one or two of the following action steps.

Display your five signature strengths. Print them out and post them in your room, create a collage that reflects them, share them on social media, or do some searches to learn more about them. Find a way to keep these strengths at the front of your mind as you connect with your friends, complete schoolwork, or do a job. The point here is to draw connections between these strengths and what you do. This will help you build your knowledge of your own strengths and become more familiar with them.

Use one of your signature strengths in a new way each day. This is a strong, research-proven activity. Choose one of your signature strengths and use it to take one small action. If you choose curiosity, you might try a new food, ask someone a question you've never asked before, or explore a new site. If you choose kindness, you might hold the door for a stranger or bring someone a coffee or a tea who wasn't expecting it. This activity will help you expand upon your best qualities.

Connect strengths with your happiness. Think of a situation in the last couple of weeks in which you were happy, engaged, and contributing in an important way. You might have been at work, with friends at school, at home on your computer, or talking with one of your parents. Write about the situation. Then take another look at the twenty-four character strengths in the survey. List at least three that you were using in this situation. This activity will help you build your strengths fluency by practicing spotting strengths in yourself.

Spot character strengths in others. In your interactions with others, think about the character strengths they seem to be using, however small. Try doing this in different situations. Find at least one character strength that the other person is displaying. Be sure to look for strengths in your parents, your siblings, your classmates, your boss, in Facebook and Instagram posts, and in the characters on TV shows or in books you're reading.

Bring strengths into your interactions with others. It's cool to talk about strengths. Talking about what's best in yourself and in others is a way to shift the conversation, to see the good in people and be able to name it, and to reframe something that isn't going so well. You can do this with your neighbors, friends, family, and social media posts.

Reflect on your role models. We all have people in our life who have inspired us. Who influences you? Who's your role model or mentor? Name a couple of people in your life who've been a positive influence. What are their top character strengths, how do they express each of those strengths, and what do you think they see in you? What character strengths do you think they would say are your signature strengths?

You're already well on your way to boosting your well-being. Now it's time to dig into each area of well-being, one by one, and unleash several powerful activities. Your happiness and resilience await!

Part 1

Manifesting Positive Vibes

Positive Emotions ➜ *Well-Being*

An important part of your well-being is recognizing and building positive emotions. It feels good to feel good! Your character strengths, such as humor, hope, and zest, can help you find the laughter, be optimistic with others, and approach life with energy and gusto. The activities in this part of the book will help you learn to create more experiences that build your positive emotions.

1 identifying positive emotions

The moment we cry in a film is not when things are sad but when they turn out to be more beautiful than we expected them to be.

—Alain de Botton

for you to know

How many times has a teacher in school asked you how you felt about a particular moment in history or political situation—or, better yet, asked you how you felt about your biology lab results or solving that proof in geometry? The truth of the matter is that there is often little room for feelings in the classroom or, for that matter, with many of the challenges you typically face. Whether you are perfecting your baseball pitch or learning a piece on the violin, there is little place for *feelings.*

This can be highly problematic, as many teens can get accustomed to pushing away feelings in favor of *thoughts.* Many times you or your friends may experience panic, tears, or anxiety seemingly out of the blue, when in reality you may have become an expert at pushing feelings down far away, and panic, tears, or anxiety may erupt from deep within you.

You can learn how to expand your emotional vocabulary to better attend to your feelings, and this is a key skill for all teens to have. Emotions can help guide important decisions that you might otherwise make just with your head, without any heart behind it. On the flip side, some teens are all too familiar with emotions and go from one high to a low and back again. This exercise will help you learn the nuances of your emotions to help you respond better in the moment.

for you to do

According to positive emotions researcher Dr. Barbara Fredrickson, there are ten core positive emotions, which are listed below. See if you can come up with examples in your life when you experienced these emotions (try to come up with examples for at least half of them). For example, you might have felt pride after you received an A on a paper you worked hard on, or you might have felt awe when you observed the night sky filled with countless stars.

Joy:_____

Love: _____

Gratitude: _____

Interest: _____

Hope: _____

Amusement: _____

Pride: _____

Awe: _____

Inspiration: _____

Desire: _____

more to do

To take things one step further, consider this artistically inspired activity! You probably are very familiar with emojis. In fact, you may find expressing feelings easier to do with images than words. Pick five positive emojis you use regularly. Draw them in the space provided. Then identify the feeling it represents with one of the ten core positive emotions, and label it with a feeling word that describes it.

the ABCs of mood 2

for you to know

One of the most common types of therapy used for helping individuals overcome anxiety, depression, and other mood concerns comes from the field of cognitive behavioral therapy (CBT). A major tenet behind CBT is that our thoughts and behaviors are closely related with our feelings. For example, if you got your grade back on a paper that you worked really hard on, and it was a D, you might feel very upset (*affect,* or feelings), you might think you (or the teacher!) are not very bright (your *cognitions,* or thoughts), and, as a result, you might not work as hard (*behavior,* or actions) the next time a paper is due. This might lead to doing even more poorly in school and reinforce a negative cycle of unhappiness. You can see in this case how feelings, thoughts, and actions are naturally related. In CBT, the goal is to break the cycle so that, ultimately, your mood and situation improve. This relationship is illustrated in figure 1:

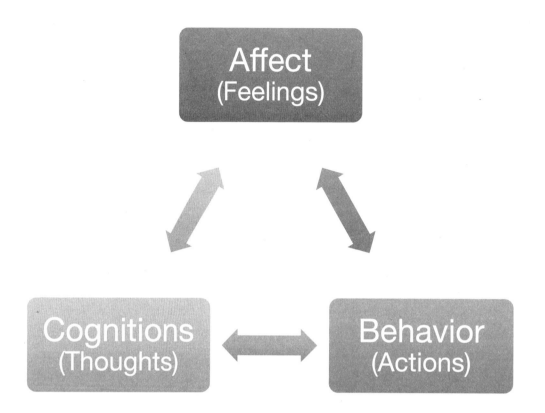

Figure 1: ABC Triangle

Looking at the example of receiving a D on a paper, you can target any part of the ABC triangle and break the negative cycle to improve your situation. Consider what Kyle did in this scenario:

Scenario: Kyle stayed up late, working for weeks on end for his English paper, but he still got a D.

A (feelings): After getting his grade, he felt defeated, upset, and frustrated. To break the cycle, Kyle could target this reaction by doing something positive.

Plan: Kyle decides to go for a jog to cool off and finds that after thirty minutes he is not nearly as upset and is feeling a bit more composed. Alternatively, he could talk to a friend in that same class and commiserate on how they both might have been unprepared for the grades they received. He may feel better by just talking with this friend.

B (actions): Getting upset that his grade was lackluster, Kyle may have punched his locker or taken out his aggression on his younger brother by yelling at him. As an alternative, he could choose a positive way of tackling this challenge through action.

Plan: Frustrated that his work on the paper was not appreciated, Kyle approaches the teacher and asks for direct feedback about what went wrong. Or he may ask for extra credit. Or if the teacher has a reputation for being particularly tough, Kyle might talk to his counselor about getting a different teacher next term or about moving to a different level that is more suited to his abilities.

C (thoughts): *I'm stupid, what is wrong with me, I hate the teacher.* Instead of finding himself in a sea of negative destructive thoughts, Kyle could follow a different plan.

Plan: Kyle chooses to focus on the areas in which he is doing well already and realizes that the D is only one grade in the context of an entire class. He could focus instead on the ways he can improve his grade in the future or even have gratitude for the other classes he is doing well in. Perhaps math is easy for him when it is a huge struggle for others.

for you to do

Now that you have a basic understanding of the ABC triangle, it's time to put this understanding into practice in your own life. Using the steps outlined in Kyle's scenario, come up with two or three scenarios from your own life (past, present, or upcoming) and write about them in the space provided. Record your feelings, actions, and thoughts within each scenario. Then reevaluate how you could break the ABC cycle by responding differently. What plans could you take to respond to your feelings, actions, and thoughts in each of these scenarios? Write about your plans in the space provided.

Scenario 1: _____

_____

_____

A (feelings): _____

_____

_____

_____

Plan: _____

_____

_____

_____

B (actions): _____

_____

_____

_____

Plan: _____

_____

_____

_____

C (thoughts): _____

_____

_____

_____

Plan: _____

_____

_____

_____

activity 2 ✳ the ABCs of mood

Scenario 2: _____

_____

_____

A (feelings): _____

_____

_____

_____

Plan: _____

_____

_____

_____

B (actions): _____

_____

_____

_____

Plan: _____

_____

_____

_____

C (thoughts): _____

_____

_____

_____

Plan: _____

_____

_____

_____

Scenario 3: _____

_____

_____

A (feelings): _____

_____

_____

_____

Plan: _____

_____

_____

_____

B (actions): _____

_____

_____

_____

Plan: _____

_____

_____

_____

C (thoughts): _____

_____

_____

_____

Plan: _____

_____

_____

_____

Remember, it takes a lot of time and practice to change your thinking and approach to things. It is very normal to be reactive when something goes wrong. It will be a challenge to take a step back and realize that most of the problems that come up can be handled with relative ease. But if you work at this, you will get better at it over time.

more to do

Friends are often the first line of defense when things go awry. You may find talking to friends on FaceTime or in the hallway helpful at times, but when your friends are constantly venting, do you find it a little overwhelming? ABC skills can come to the rescue! As you continue practicing ABC skills with your own challenges, see if you can't offer this same simple concept to your friends when a problem comes up for them. Teaching something is, after all, one of the best ways we really learn it ourselves. Write down a scenario in which you can help a friend break the ABC cycle using the steps you've learned.

Friend's scenario: _____

_____

_____

A (feelings): _____

_____

_____

Plan: _____

_____

_____

_____

B (actions): _____

_____

_____

activity 2 ✳ the ABCs of mood

Plan: _____

_____

_____

_____

C (thoughts): _____

_____

_____

Plan: _____

_____

_____

_____

forecasting your mood 3

Our inability to recall how we really felt is why our wealth of experiences turns out to be poverty of riches.

—Daniel Gilbert

for you to know

Think back to a major event in your life that you spent months anticipating. Maybe it was getting your driver's license, your first homecoming or prom, a first kiss, or first crush. Was it everything you had been imagining, or were the actual circumstances different from what you had imagined? Maybe the dance wasn't as fun as you thought it might be, or even though you did pass your driver's test, you almost got into a collision on the test drive. Or perhaps everything went smoothly, and you were in bliss for weeks. Then something happened and the magic slowly died down, only to be replaced by new anticipation or stressors of life.

The idea of *affective forecasting* is an important concept in happiness research. It describes how we each predict what we will feel in a given scenario. Have you ever said to yourself, *If this thing happens, I'll never want anything again?* Chances are that if your desire came true, after a few weeks or even months, you got used to this new normal and were no longer as thrilled as you thought you would be. This is what scientists often call *hedonic adaptation,* the idea that we always return to our previous emotional state after a major event. This can relate to both positive and negative events. For example, if you ever bombed an exam, you may have been devastated at first, but were you back to normal after a few weeks?

Learning to identify errors in your thinking and prediction of events can be a powerful way of reframing events and checking your expectations, whether you are super excited about something that's going to happen or are stressing over it. As many teenagers report (and as their parents experience with them), moods can often feel like a roller coaster ride. One day everything is going amazing, and the next it feels like everything is crashing down. By taking a step back and comparing these highs and lows to your previous experiences, you can learn to take charge of your emotions and finally get off the emotional roller coaster!

for you to do

Take out your planner, calendar, or phone and find some key life events that happened over the last several months. Maybe you've already forgotten about the beach trip you took a month ago or the SAT exam you were dreading for the last six months. List two scenarios: one negative event and one positive event. Then, use the rating scale of 1 to 5 provided, circle how you thought the event would impact your mood, how it actually impacted your mood, and how you feel now that the event is in the past. First look at the sample provided:

Sample negative scenario: *Taking the ACT exam, which I experienced as being a highly stressful scenario*

Anticipated Mood

Highly stressful	Somewhat stressful	Neutral	Positive	Highly positive
(1)	2	3	4	5

Actual Impact on Mood

Highly stressful	Somewhat stressful	Neutral	Positive	Highly positive
(1)	2	3	4	5

Current Mood Regarding Past Scenario

Highly stressful	Somewhat stressful	Neutral	Positive	Highly positive
1	2	(3)	4	5

Now come up with a negative and a positive scenario in your own life. Then rate the impact on your mood before and during the events and the impact that these events have on your mood now.

Negative scenario: _____

Anticipated Mood

Highly stressful	Somewhat stressful	Neutral	Positive	Highly positive
1	2	3	4	5

Actual Impact on Mood

Highly stressful	Somewhat stressful	Neutral	Positive	Highly positive
1	2	3	4	5

Current Mood Regarding Past Scenario

Highly stressful	Somewhat stressful	Neutral	Positive	Highly positive
1	2	3	4	5

Positive scenario: _____

Anticipated Mood

Highly stressful	Somewhat stressful	Neutral	Positive	Highly positive
1	2	3	4	5

Actual Impact on Mood

Highly stressful	Somewhat stressful	Neutral	Positive	Highly positive
1	2	3	4	5

Current Mood Regarding Past Scenario

Highly stressful	Somewhat stressful	Neutral	Positive	Highly positive
1	2	3	4	5

more to do

After looking at some past scenarios, see if you can use what you've learned to better forecast events coming up in the future. What about your experience can help with both your anticipation and your experience of major events? For this next exercise, list one positive scenario—an event you are looking forward to or are very excited about— and one negative scenario, something which you are not looking forward to. Using the rating scale of 1 to 5 provided, circle how you think each event will impact your mood, and then brainstorm some ideas on how to reappraise the two scenarios. Hint: By acknowledging that things may not turn out exactly the way you think, you can begin to get off the emotional roller coaster.

Sample positive scenario: For my birthday, my parents are letting me go to a concert with a friend to see my favorite band. It's going to be the highlight of sophomore year.

Anticipated Mood

Highly stressful	Somewhat stressful	Neutral	Positive	Highly positive
1	2	3	(4)	5

Reappraisal: The event will definitely be fun and I'm very excited. In addition to the anticipation, I'm going to focus on savoring the experience and having gratitude for this amazing gift. I'm also going to be prepared that it is possible not everything is going to go according to a perfect plan, and I will know that's okay.

Positive scenario: _____

Anticipated Mood

Highly stressful	Somewhat stressful	Neutral	Positive	Highly positive
1	2	3	4	5

Reappraisal: _____

_____

Negative scenario: _____

Anticipated Mood

Highly stressful	Somewhat stressful	Neutral	Positive	Highly positive
1	2	3	4	5

Reappraisal: _____

_____

_____

_____

4   happiness (zest booster!)

True happiness…is not attained through self-gratification but through fidelity to a worthy purpose.

—Helen Keller

for you to know

Researchers studying the concept of happiness often refer to it as satisfaction with life. Through describing it this way, they have come up with a simple way of measuring and studying happiness and its relationship with hundreds of variables.

Happiness can also be thought of as a destination or as a journey. For example, philosophers talk about pleasure-based activities *(hedonia)* and engagement or meaning-based *(eudaimonia)* as different routes to happiness. Seeking pleasure, you might be focused on material possessions, wealth, food, alcohol, and romantic relationships, but never feel satisfied. Another way to find happiness is in focusing on helping others, kindness, intellectually challenging yourself, or growing spiritually.

for you to do

Check out this "Satisfaction with Life Scale," created by pioneering positive psychologist Ed Diener and colleagues in 1985. Rate how much you agree or disagree with these statements by filling in the blank next to each statement with a number on the following scale of 1 to 7, where 1 is strongly disagree, 2 is disagree, 3 is slightly disagree, 4 is neither agree nor disagree, 5 is slightly agree, 6 is agree, and 7 is strongly agree.

Please be open and honest as you respond.

_____ *In most ways my life is close to my ideal.*

_____ *The conditions of my life are excellent.*

_____ *I am satisfied with my life.*

_____ *So far, I have gotten the important things I want in life.*

_____ *If I could live my life over, I would change almost nothing.*

Scoring: Add up your numbers. Here are some benchmarks to give you a sense of your general satisfaction with life.

31–35: Extremely satisfied

26–30: Satisfied

21–25: Slightly satisfied

20: Neutral

15–19: Slightly dissatisfied

10–14: Dissatisfied

5–9: Extremely dissatisfied

more to do

Five character strengths have been connected to happiness across many studies of people across countries, ages, and backgrounds. These five *happiness strengths* are zest, hope, gratitude, curiosity, and love. Researchers have found that 75 percent of us possess at least one of these as a signature strength, which is excellent news for enhancing happiness!

You can also enhance these strengths to boost your overall happiness, even if none of them appears among your top five. Look at each of the following ways to enhance your happiness strengths. Then come up with two more activities for each one and consider integrating them into your week!

Zest:

1. Exercise! Get moving and feel the endorphins flowing.

2. _____

3. _____

Hope:

1. Create a vision board or list of goals you are hoping to achieve over the next year or even decade. Keep this list or these images in a place where you can see them and be inspired.

2. _____

3. _____

Gratitude:

1. Thank a teacher, coach, or parent that you may have wanted to thank before but never got around to. It can be in person, via email, letter, or even a quick text. Say thank you with genuine authenticity and heart.

2. _____

3. _____

Curiosity:

1. Go outside on a clear night and look up at the sky. See if you can identify a particular star, constellation, or a planet. Google what might be in the sky that night and see if you can find it in the stars!

2. _____

3. _____

Love:

1. Express caring and loving attention to another person, animal, or living thing. Maybe you water your plants and weed them thoughtfully or play with or feed a pet. Or, if you have a younger sibling, you attend to him or her with gentle loving attention.

2. _____

3. _____

5 optimism (hope booster!)

I believe any success in life is made by going into an area with a blind, furious optimism.

—Sylvester Stallone

for you to know

Some people like to say that optimism is simply seeing the glass half full versus seeing it half empty. However, optimism isn't just about your perspective on life. It's linked to far-reaching implications for your health and emotional well-being, from helping with recovery from surgery to reducing stress levels.

There are two main ways researchers describe optimism. The first is *dispositional optimism,* which refers to a general worldview or tendency to see things as positive and hopeful. Those who are low on dispositional optimism may tend to be pessimistic about things. You might have even heard someone described as having a "sunny disposition." This nicely captures the idea of dispositional optimism.

Explanatory optimism, on the other hand, is a little more complicated, as it refers to how people explains things that happen in their life. Such explanations are typically personal, permanent, and pervasive.

1. *Personal* explanations can be either *internal* or *external,* which is the difference between saying *I got an F because I'm a bad student* (an internal explanation) and *I got an A because I worked hard* (an external explanation).

2. *Permanent* explanations can refer to *stable* (fixed or inflexible) or *unstable* (changeable or malleable) traits. Example: *I got a C on the quiz because I'm just bad at tests* (stable trait) versus *I got a C on the quiz because I didn't study hard enough* (unstable trait).

3. *Pervasive* can take the form of thinking in terms of either global trends or more specific beliefs. *Teachers generally hate students and want them to do poorly on exams* is an example of a global belief, whereas *I've experienced teachers generally to be committed to helping students do well and succeed* is a specific belief.

Research suggests those with an internal, unstable, and global explanatory style tend to be more susceptible to depression; they possess a pessimistic explanatory style. Those with an external, stable, and specific explanatory style tend to be more resilient; they possess an optimistic explanatory style.

for you to do

Below, come up with an example of a time when something happened and you interpreted it through an optimistic explanatory style, and come up with a second scenario where you may have fallen victim to a pessimistic explanatory style. For the pessimistic explanatory style, see if you can come up with a new modified interpretation to view what happened more positively (see scenario 2 reframe).

Scenario 1 (optimistic explanatory style): _____

_____

_____

Personal (external explanation):_____

_____

Permanent (unstable trait):_____

_____

Pervasive (specific belief):_____

_____

Scenario 2 (pessimistic explanatory style): _____

_____

_____

Personal (internal explanation): _____

_____

Permanent (stable trait): _____

_____

Pervasive (global trend): _____

_____

Scenario 2 reframe (optimistic explanatory style): _____

_____

_____

Personal (external explanation): _____

_____

Permanent (unstable trait): _____

_____

Pervasive (specific belief): _____

_____

more to do

As you may have already guessed, the signature character strength most associated with optimism is hope. Focusing on manifesting hope can be done in countless ways! Three areas to consider include school/career, friends/relationships, and parents/family (feel free to add sports, volunteer, or other activities you may consider a large part of your life). Take some time to brainstorm an action in which you might involve hope to instill a greater sense of optimism in each of these areas. Fill in your own examples underneath the examples that are provided in each category.

School/career: *To obtain my goal of graduating with honors, I will diligently use my planner and set aside extra time to study every day.*

_____

_____

_____

Friends/relationships: *Given that I often feel lonely and underappreciated at school, I will join new clubs in the hope of meeting new people who I may be able to connect with on a deeper level.*

_____

_____

_____

Parents/family: *I often feel like the problem child among my siblings. I will aim to do my chores the first time I am asked and chip in on additional tasks such as filling the dishwasher to show I am trying to contribute more to our household.*

_____

_____

_____

LOL and live fully (humor booster!) 6

Always laugh when you can. It is cheap medicine.

—Lord Byron

for you to know

Studies suggest that fifteen minutes of laughter a day can burn between ten to forty calories depending upon the individual's weight and intensity of laughter! But perhaps even more important, laughter has been shown to reduce blood pressure, increase T cells (which help ward off illness), release endorphins, and reduce stress hormones.

Finding the humor in life is certainly a strength that comes naturally to many teens, sometimes to the frustration of teachers and parents. It is likely you and your friends often tease each other, laugh over YouTube clips, or generally goof off at times without too many cares about worries or stressors. On the other hand, you might be so overwhelmed with school and activities that laughter seems to come all too rarely. Wherever you fall on this continuum, you have likely experienced just how cathartic a really good laugh can be. Maybe it's from a funny movie or maybe from slipping on a banana peel and then laughing over the silliness of it all.

for you to do

Playfulness is one of the foundations of humor. Gentle teasing and even (appropriate) self-deprecation can set the tone for giggles and laughter. It is important, of course, to be mindful of the impact of your humor use, as the same joke might bring laughter to one person, feelings of anger to another, and feelings of devastation, hurt, or upset to someone else. Below are some questions to get you thinking about how you might integrate more humor into your life:

What are some of the ways you initiate playfulness at home, school, or other social contexts?

_____

_____

_____

Do you find yourself being more open to using humor with certain friend groups or people than with others? If so, with whom? How might you express humor with more people?

_____

_____

_____

When have you used humor appropriately to diffuse a stressful situation? Give an example.

_____

_____

_____

When might you have missed the mark, and your humor was hurtful to others? Given an example.

_____

_____

_____

What are some simple ways you might focus on increasing humor in your everyday life?

_____

_____

_____

more to do

To continue to integrate more humor into your life, consider these options. Check off those that you might want to try, and add your own ideas at the bottom of the list:

☐ Keep a list of funny movies that always make you laugh so you can watch when you're in need of a good belly laugh.

☐ Try out a new silly activity that will leave you in stitches. Maybe it is a Zumba or other dance class where you may feel silly and laugh in response.

☐ Find a YouTube channel focused around comedy as a go-to option when you want a good laugh.

☐ Make it a habit to share jokes, funny memes, or clips with friends to create an overall culture of levity so you can support one another during challenging times.

☐ Find a laughter yoga class. Yes, these exist!

☐ Consider taking a stand-up comedy class or just attend stand-up comedy shows.

☐ Each classroom typically has a class clown. Consider observing or befriending that person to see what works for them and what doesn't.

Add your own ideas here:

_____

_____

_____

_____

how positive emotions can relieve mental stress

7

When we long for life without difficulties, remind us that oaks grow strong in contrary winds and diamonds are made under pressure.

—Peter Marshall

for you to know

According to the National Institutes of Health, over 30 percent of teens have a diagnosable anxiety disorder. Further, the American Psychological Association reports that 59 percent of teens find that balancing all of their competing demands leads to stress. It is no wonder then that so many teens are looking for ways to better manage their stress levels.

As a teen, you may already be aware of the host of ways you and your friends manage stress. You may choose healthy coping mechanisms such as exercise and connecting with friends for support. Better yet, you and your friends might talk to a school counselor from time to time or seek professional help from a mental health professional. On the flip side, you may know teens who engage in risky behaviors, such as drugs and alcohol, to cope. The good news is that there are plenty of ways to use positive emotions to help you cope in trying times.

for you to do

Here are some coping tools that may provide some relief when you are experiencing difficult emotions. Place a check mark next to the ones you'd like to try and an X next to the steps you are less interested in:

☐ **Consider perspective.** See if you can tap into your perspective strength to get a more neutral view of the problem you are experiencing. Imagine you were an outside observer. What would you see? Getting some perspective may help you see that one bad grade or perceived failure may not be as bad as you initially think.

☐ **Get zesty!** Zest is a natural strength that can be a great resource, even if you don't feel it in the present moment. Try coming up with a list of adventures and plans for the future to help get you out of a funk in the present. Maybe you have been wanting to go for a hike for a long time or simply wanting to try out that new ice cream shop with quirky flavors. Or you may want to plan to enroll in a spinning class on Saturday before it fills up. There are plenty of ways to bring more zest into your day, week, and weekends!

☐ **Remember to laugh!** Revisit activity 6 and your list of ways to add laughter to your life. Whether it is watching silly YouTube clips or a funny movie, finding a way to laugh every day is an excellent way of destressing.

☐ **Say "Namaste" or "Amen"!** Spirituality is highly correlated with a sense of meaning and peace. Further, a sense of spirituality can help you access your gratitude strength through showing you that you already have so much to be grateful for in your life. Whether it is going to a yoga class, attending a church group or service, or communing with nature, accessing your spiritual side can do wonders for lowering stress. After expressing your spiritual side in whatever way you choose, consider bowing your head and silently saying *thank you* for the incredible experience.

more to do

You might consider using a *thought log* to help you reframe your automatic thoughts. Look at the example that follows. Then use the space that follows to make your own thought log. First write down a stressful or challenging event that you have recently experienced or are currently going through. In the *automatic thoughts* column, write down the thoughts and feelings you are having about this situation. If you have conflicting thoughts and emotions, that's okay! The goal is to just get it all down on paper. In the next column, list any character strengths that might help you combat these thoughts or emotions. In the final column, reframe your thoughts based on your character strengths. You can also download this worksheet for future use at http://www.newharbinger.com/46028.

Stressful scenario: Taking the SAT exam this weekend.

Feelings	Automatic Thoughts	Helpful Character Strengths	Reframing with Character Strengths
Anxiety	What if I fail?	Perspective	Perspective: This is only one exam in the big picture of my life. Even if it doesn't go well, I can retake it.
Worry	I'm not smart enough.	Optimism	
Fear			The SAT is only one factor in college admissions. It's a privilege to even be considering college as an option when many cannot.
Sadness	I'm bad at tests.		
Concern			Optimism: I might get an "easy" version of the test, and it might not go as poorly as I thought.

Reframing Automatic Thoughts

Stressful scenario:

Feelings	Automatic Thoughts	Helpful Character Strengths	Reframing with Character Strengths

Part 2

Finding the Flow of Your Life

Your Engagement → Well-Being

Feeling engaged and connected with what you are doing is an important part of your well-being. Whether you are in the zone on the basketball court, listening closely to a teacher, or reading a book, when feeling engaged, you are usually at your best in that moment. Your strengths of curiosity, creativity, and leadership can help you engage more in whatever you are doing. The activities in this section will help you find that engagement you've been looking for.

8 what motivates you?

Education is not the filling of a bucket but the lighting of a fire.

—W. B. Yeats

for you to know

Let's say you want to get more Facebook likes or Instagram followers, win a school award, graduate from school, have tons of views of a video you posted, go to a concert by one of your favorite bands, hang out after school with friends, or get a new video game. These are all examples of *extrinsic motivation,* which makes you want to work hard, get your homework done, stick with your classes, and reach your goals. But sometimes external things are not the strongest motivators you have. If you want to be successful in the long run, you need to ignite your internal motivators.

Internal motivators are found inside you, in contrast with the kinds of motivators just mentioned, which all lie outside of you. With intrinsic motivation, you follow your inner strengths, use your curiosity, challenge yourself, and focus on what lights you up. Research has found that intrinsic motivation is solidly rooted in your brain and helps you develop in learning, performance, creativity, and general well-being.

Ask yourself: *What am I naturally good at that also poses a challenge for me? What do I like to do even though it involves effort? What do I most like to learn?* Answering these questions will offer you your own personal recipe for your intrinsic motivation.

It might be that you feel both challenged and excited to learn a new language or you love to learn by reading about wild animals from different countries or you love studying how-to videos on YouTube. Pursuing the things you love, are curious about, and that challenge you will motivate you in your life.

for you to do

Is there a change that you have been wanting to make but are needing a bit of a push? Maybe you want to approach that guy or girl you are attracted to? Maybe you want to cut down on your late-night snacking? Maybe you want to quit smoking or spend less time online? Maybe you want to be a better team player or practice your musical instrument more? Intrinsic motivation is about pushing yourself! Try these steps to give yourself that extra push you need. Below each suggestion, write down how you could use this character strength to make changes for the better.

1. Use your *perspective* to consider one change or action you want to take. Stepping back from your situation, ask yourself how you would benefit from taking action.

   _____

   _____

   _____

2. Use your *curiosity* to explore these questions: What is one thing you might discover if you take this action? What might you explore in yourself, another person, or a situation as you take action?

   _____

   _____

   _____

3. Use your *bravery* to move out of your comfort zone by taking one step toward making a change. What is the first step you'll be taking?

_____

_____

_____

4. After you take action, use your *love of learning* to consider what you learned from your experience. Also use this strength to think about what you would do differently the next time, if anything.

_____

_____

_____

Using your perspective, curiosity, bravery, and love of learning, you now have a process for building your motivation!

more to do

Try some of these motivation strategies that have helped many others locate their inner spark.

- Pause for a moment to ask yourself this: *If I could learn about anything today, what would it be?* Take action to learn about this topic by discussing it with someone who knows about it, by reading a book about it, or by searching for insights online.

- Motivate yourself to take on a new challenge by considering the greater good it will bring to you or others. Maybe by persevering with your school assignment, you'll be building knowledge that you can later use to help others. By participating in the school play, you'll be building up your character strength of bravery. Acting in front of others might spur your confidence in other situations where you will need courage.

- Name a time when you enjoyed working hard on something; maybe it was a school project, personal training, or a piece of music or art. Notice how you felt. Notice how you were in the flow of that experience. Remember that feeling and experience of natural inner motivation the next time you want inspiration.

9 getting in the flow

The best moments in our lives are not the passive, receptive, relaxing times… The best moments usually occur if a person's body or mind is stretched to its limits in a voluntary effort to accomplish something difficult and worthwhile.

—Mihaly Csikszentmihalyi

for you to know

Many athletes instantaneously know that feeling they get when they are in the zone—that sense when time disappears, any physical pain subsides, and you are fully immersed in what you are doing. Artists know this feeling well when they are so taken by their painting or pottery that the hours just go by without any awareness of time at all. Musicians and composers get fully lost in their craft as well. This phenomenon has a name coined by legendary psychologist Dr. Mihaly Csikszentmihalyi. It is called *flow,* a state of complete mental absorption with the activity at hand.

Flow is commonly understood to have several components:

- Total concentration on the task at hand

- Clear goals and a mental reward as well as immediate feedback

- A sense of losing the existence of time (time seems to speed up or slow down)

- An intrinsically rewarding component to the experience

- Effort and ease whereby the challenge of the task is matched with the skills needed to perform it

Visually, the experience of flow is depicted in figure 2 as the point where level of skill is matched with level of challenge. You may also notice that anxiety lives in the place where the skills are low relative to the challenge level (such as taking that AP Calculus class that might have you biting your nails); and boredom occurs when the skill and challenge level are both low (reading a history book written in a monotonous and uninspired way).

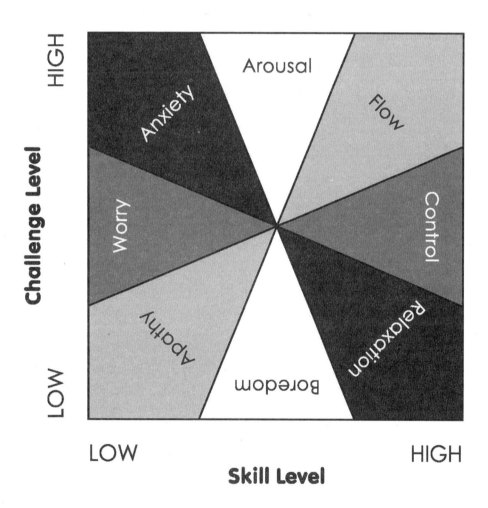

Figure 2: Flow Theory

for you to do

Get out a pencil and set a timer for five minutes for this next exercise. In the space provided, jot down all of the times or activities you remember getting lost in the flow. Maybe you were at band practice or in your room cartooning. If you need an extra boost of inspiration, consider taking a quick look at some recent photos on your phone or peruse an old journal to help you recall your accomplishments and what you enjoy doing most. Let your mind wander and let the inspiration flow!

_____

_____

_____

_____

_____

more to do

Now that you have spent some time reacquainting yourself with what flow looks like for you, it's time to put this into action. Pick two or three of the activities you listed in the previous exercise and see if you can't make time over the next week to practice these things. To keep yourself accountable, list the activities under the flow column and then place an X next to the day when you plan to do this activity in the coming week:

Flow Activity	Sun	Mon	Tues	Wed	Thurs	Fri	Sat

At the end of the week, spend a few minutes writing about how things went. What feelings did you experience most during your flow activities?

_____

_____

_____

_____

10 engage with your signature strengths

Knowing yourself is the beginning of all wisdom.

—Aristotle

for you to know

Remember the signature strengths test you completed at the beginning of this book? Have you memorized your signature strengths, your top five? It's good to keep your best qualities at the top of your mind and ready for use at any time. Your signature strengths can likely be described with five Es:

Essential. These strengths describe who you are, at your core.

Energizing. You feel uplifted when you use them.

Easy. These strengths come natural to you, flow right out of you. You just have to remember to use them!

Exciting. You feel excitement and joy using them.

Engaging. You are connected with what you are doing when you use them.

You can use your signature strengths to help you reach your goals, develop a new relationship, get your homework done, or feel a greater sense of meaning in your life. This activity will focus on using your signature strengths to engage more in your daily life.

for you to do

Take a look at the example in the following signature strengths worksheet, and then write down your signature strengths and one or two ways you have used each of these strengths in the recent past. Keep the five Es in mind as you look for times that were energizing, exciting, and engaging, or when you felt like you were expressing the real you. Write about how you felt using your strengths and how you will use these strengths this week.

Doing this activity will help build your awareness of your signature strengths. You might consider plugging your ideas for the week into your smart device and refreshing them weekly. This will help you keep using your strengths in new ways, therefore expanding your possibilities for positive action. You can also download the worksheet for future use at http://www.newharbinger.com/46028.

Signature Strengths Worksheet

Ranking	Signature Strength	One to Two Ways You've Used This Strength Recently	How You Felt Using This Strength	How You Will Use This Strength This Week
Example:	Social intelligence	I asked my friend how they were feeling. And I noticed a tense argument between my mom and dad, so I decided to just observe first.	I felt at peace, like I was in control and able to take action to help others.	Before I post new photos online, I will first think about how others might feel when they see them.
1.				
2.				

3.	4.	5.

more to do

It is easy for your strengths to slip from your mind. You're busy with school, friends, family, relationships, sports, extracurricular activities, hobbies, and much more. But remember, you can bring who you are—your signature strengths—into any situation.

Can you think of some new ways to keep your signature strengths on the top of your mind? Here are two stories that may inspire you.

- *Jacob's Story*

  Jacob was a nineteen-year-old who was surprised to learn that curiosity was a signature strength that he could use. It made sense to him on one level, but it was new for him to really endorse this as a central part of his character. Then he became curious about new ways he could use his curiosity! He wanted to bring greater curiosity into his daily routines, and to remind himself, he made a simple lamination with his signature strengths and placed it on the back of his phone, which he takes everywhere. At his part-time job, Jacob is on his computer much of the time, so he created a backdrop on his screen with five quotes, one for each of his signature strengths. With these strategies, he knew he would be inspired to express his best qualities regularly.

- *April's Story*

  A fifteen-year-old named April was excited by her signature strengths. These were positive labels that accurately described who she felt she really was! She wanted to share this with others in a creative way, so she went online searching for the best images to capture each of her five signature strengths. She printed up an image or a photo for each of them, which she then assembled into a pretty collage. For example, she had a mountain landscape to represent her appreciation of beauty, a photo of her parents hugging to represent love, and a picture of herself rock climbing to show perseverance. She posted the collage on social media and taped it on the inside of her locker and on her bedroom wall for inspiration.

How will you keep your signature strengths in the forefront of your mind? Write down your plan and then take action!

_____

_____

_____

_____

_____

11 commit random acts of kindness

My religion is very simple. My religion is kindness.

—His Holiness the Dalai Lama

for you to know

Have you heard of the pay-it-forward effect? This means that kind acts can be contagious and that they are beneficial for the person expressing kindness as well as the receiver of the kindness. There are so many ways to be kind: you can strike up a conversation with a classmate who is sitting alone, give your friend a compliment for one of his strengths, help your mother or father out on a household project, call one of your grandparents on the phone, help your neighbor rake her leaves, or give a small gift to someone "just because."

One research study showed that kindness can cascade through your network to three degrees of separation. In other words, it's possible that your kindness can spread to the friends of your friend's friends! Think about that for a moment. Your simple act of kindness can cause a positive ripple and bring benefit to many people you've never even met!

In a study involving nine- to eleven-year-olds, the kids were asked to perform three acts of kindness each day. Compared to a group of kids who did not participate, the group who expressed kindness experienced a lift in their well-being as well as a boost to their acceptance by their peers. We encourage you to practice this activity. You might come to realize what so many others have discovered: it's fun to be kind!

for you to do

Make kindness simple. Make it easy. Make it yours. Don't think about it too much. All you have to do is focus on others, listen to them and what they might need, and take action. That's kindness.

Think of one way you might show kindness to one or more people today that would benefit them. Write it down here. Be sure that you're not taking the action to win points or to receive a favor from them later.

_____

_____

_____

Set up a reminder to yourself each morning to plan to deliberately commit a kind act each day. What time will you set the reminder for? How does that time make sense to you? Note that the key here is not to do a big act of kindness each day but to get into a regular routine of being kind.

_____

_____

_____

Mix up your kind acts. Sometimes you might just seize the moment, other times you might kindly react in a situation, and other times you might plan ahead. Mixing it up like this will make kindness feel authentic rather than forced or contrived.

more to do

You can build off this activity with another action called the gift of time. This action opens the door to building connections with others. Here's how it goes:

1. Name three people in your life whom you could support, cheer up, or help by spending time with them this week. Be sure to think of people whom you would not otherwise have seen or connected with this week.

   _____

   _____

2. Take action and selflessly give one of them your time. How will you use your signature strengths when you are with this person?

   _____

   _____

3. After you take action, reflect on your experience and theirs.

   _____

   _____

While it is clear that this activity benefits others, researchers have found that the person giving the gift of time can experience significant boosts in their happiness and decreases in depression.

use your strengths to 12
engage your mind and heart

The mind strengthens the heart, one is ruled by reason and the other by raw emotion, but together they build us into something beautiful: a human being.

—Amanda de los Santos

for you to know

Your character strengths can be expressed through your mind or your heart. Some strengths like judgment, prudence, and creativity are more *mind oriented.* They involve logic, thinking, and analysis. You might use prudence to think through a plan for the weekend or creativity to think about many ways to solve a problem you're having at school. Other strengths are reflected more by your feelings, senses, and intuitions, and are especially *heart oriented.* Typical examples include gratitude, love, and kindness. You might express heartfelt gratitude to a friend who supported you after you lost your tennis match or love to your mother with a warm hug.

While each of your strengths might lean more toward the heart or the mind, it's possible to express any strength in your thoughts or your feelings. For example, you can have loving thoughts about someone, and you can feel the uplifting energy of zest in your body when you are excited about seeing one of your friends.

In different situations, it can help to be more mind focused or more heart focused. When doing math problems, you might want to be more mind focused, but when writing an essay you might choose to write from the heart. In each situation, you can weigh your options and then turn to your character strengths to help you.

for you to do

Let's put this into action.

1. Name a problem or stressor.

    Example: Feeling lonely on Friday night when my peers seem to be out having fun.

    _____

    _____

2. Choose one of your signature strengths to help you address the difficulty.

    Example: creativity

    _____

3. How might you use this signature strength in a mind-oriented way, from a place of thinking and logic?

    Example: I can use my creativity to brainstorm several things I can do for fun tonight, such as picking out a movie I've wanted to see, learning a new game like chess or Sudoku, making some comments on Instagram, and calling a friend or a relative I haven't spoken with in a while.

    _____

    _____

4. How might you use this signature strength in a heart-focused way, from a place of feelings?

Example: I'll explore what could help me feel creative. Then I'll do something to be productive, like I'm getting something new accomplished. Some ideas I have are to create a video that tells a story about someone overcoming isolation or to write a poem about loneliness.

_____

_____

5. Review what you came up with for numbers three and four, and decide on one way to take action with your strength right away.

_____

_____

Your strengths will help you engage your heart and mind. They'll help you tackle life challenges in new ways and support you in taking a well-rounded approach.

more to do

Consider a conflict you are having with someone in your life. Engage your mind and heart with these strength-based questions and strategies. Choose the approach that might best help you in this particular situation.

Judgment. Use your critical thinking skills to think outside the box with a problem. What is a way to solve the problem that you've never considered before?

Social intelligence. As you think about the conflict, attend to the feelings of yourself and others. Is there an appropriate way to share your feelings in the situation? How might you empathize with how others are feeling?

Appreciation of beauty. Step away from the conflict for a moment to refresh yourself with beauty. Look for beauty in one of three things: nature, art, or acts of goodness by others. Allow yourself to be filled with the beauty you observe. Feel it fully before you return to thinking about the conflict.

Perspective. Allow your view of the conflict to widen. How would a wise person in your life approach the problem?

Creativity. Give yourself creativity space. Set aside a period of time to be creative to solve or handle the conflict. Don't judge what you come up with, but allow your creativity to be unleashed.

Fairness. Approach the conflict using the lens of fairness. What is fair in this situation for both you and the other person? What is the fairest way to handle it for all concerned?

I have no special talents. I am only passionately curious.

—Albert Einstein

for you to know

We live in a world that is often fast paced, vibrant, and full of potential for immediate action. People are constantly reinventing themselves, or at least renewing themselves, with social media pictures and videos. It may seem like everyone around you is engaging in new, fun activities. This may make you feel like everything should be interesting, engaging, and exciting. When that does not happen, life can feel tedious, slow paced, and dull. It is easy to feel bored.

Do you want to know the trick for overcoming boredom? It's novelty. When you look for something novel, unique, or new in a situation, your brain becomes active. It begins to search and explore. This is the opposite effect of vegging out, sitting back lost in thought or fantasy or being on autopilot. Novelty seeking is rooted in your natural strength of curiosity.

Are you active or passive with your curiosity? How can you know? Well, if you are passively curious, you are reacting to something in your environment. You see a hummingbird suddenly fly in your backyard, notice someone on the street who is dressed in provocative clothing, or take note when someone brings up a fact you've never heard. These are examples in which you are reacting to someone or something else. This is passive curiosity.

But you can also be actively curious, which is when you are in the driver's seat. You might be genuinely interested in how your friend did at his performance over the weekend, so you ask him questions. You might be intrigued by Komodo dragons, so you begin to watch Netflix documentaries and search online for information about these creatures that live only in Indonesia. You might be curious to explore your emotions after a tumultuous weekend of friendship, betrayal, and new connections, and so you decide to journal about your experiences. These are all examples of active curiosity, and it feels great!

for you to do

Ready to become actively curious? Try out these steps:

1. Choose any activity that you don't like to do or one that you usually quickly become bored doing. It might be doing the dishes, waiting in line at the store, cleaning your room, folding your laundry, getting gas for your car, driving to work, mowing your yard, or talking to someone you don't particularly like. Write down one of these activities that usually bores you.

   _____

2. When you do this activity this week, pay attention to three novel (or unique) features of the activity *while you are doing it.* See if any of your senses will help you connect with the activity. Pay attention to the details. For example, if you are doing the dishes, you may notice the warmth of the soapy water, the fresh scent arising from the bubbles, and the sound of water gurgling as it drains. What do you notice that you typically do not see or hear? Try to experience the activity in a new and fresh way.

3. Write down your experiences or discuss them with a friend this week.

   _____

   _____

   _____

   _____

   _____

Here's an example of how being actively curious can change things.

● *Sharon's Story*

Sharon noticed she was lost in her routine on Facebook. She would review the same streams, "like" most things she spent more than a couple seconds on, and would post a couple of the same kind of comments each time she logged in. This had become such a mindless routine that she often felt bored by it. She decided to apply active curiosity to look for new details in Facebook posts by her friends that she and others would have usually overlooked, such as someone smirking in the background, the colored patterns on one of the shirts, and the contours of the environment. She then wrote curious questions in her comments, often pointing out novel features and enjoying herself much more.

more to do

Want more boredom-crushing tips? Try these strategies to help you connect with and engage in the present moment.

- **Do something different.** Make this your motto when you feel boredom on the rise. What is something different you could do or say or a different way to think right now?

- **Move, move, move.** Oftentimes when boredom strikes, we are sitting around, waiting for life to happen. Counteract this by getting up and walking, going for a jog, putting on some rollerblades, shooting baskets, dancing, or moving in another way that will get your body (and brain) going.

- **Photograph boredom.** Take a picture of your boredom (how you are sitting, what you are doing) and post it. You'll probably laugh doing it and amuse others too. Suddenly, you have turned your boredom into a funny, engaging experience.

Part 3

Developing a Drama-Free (and Happy) Tribe

Positive Relationships → Well-Being

Creating good relationships with others where there's a balance of give and take is pivotal in boosting your well-being. Turn to your strengths of love, kindness, and teamwork to help you bring not only your attention but also your thoughtfulness and care to others. The activities in this section will support you on this journey of improving your connection with everyone in your life: friends, boyfriend or girlfriend, coworkers, classmates, siblings, and parents.

14 next-level bully management

for you to know

Bullying is an increasingly problematic behavior for teens worldwide. Studies indicate that 70 percent of students have seen bullying occur at their own schools and that another 30 percent of teens admit to bullying others. Further, with the popularity of social media, much of bullying has been translated to the cyberworld, making it even more incessant and harder for adults to intervene. A bully can be anyone—large or small—and bullying behavior can range from serious physical threats to playful teasing that appears aggressive only to the person being bullied.

Learning to take a step back before problems escalate is a challenge for anyone. After all, it is natural to want to react immediately by fighting or running away when you are feeling upset about something. However, stopping to take a deep breath and consider your options, possibly talking through your feelings with a friend or parent, can help you get the space you need before you respond. This is where tapping into your prudence strength can be incredibly powerful. Prudence can help you access your inner wisdom to avoid unnecessary conflict, exercise caution, and develop your planning skills as you think of peaceful solutions. And prudence may help kids who bully to think before they act and limit their aggressiveness. Tapping prudence is like channeling your inner Dumbledore, Gandalf, or Yoda! What do these characters do when confronted with dark forces? They go inward and from a place of peace and stillness are able to tackle the problem with incredible peaceful strength far more powerful than any aggressive attack they may encounter!

for you to do

Depending on your unique situation, you may already be in the midst of dealing with a bully, helping a friend overwhelmed by one, or seeing bullying in the hallways on a regular basis. While you need not feel obligated to jump into a superhero mode and go around rescuing everyone, you can start by running through this checklist the next time you are confronted with bullying. Following these suggestions will help you build up your prudence strength and support you in feeling more confident to handle the situation.

Speak up. The first thing to do when you are being bullied or witnessing bullying is to report it. While the goal is not to be a snitch or to try to get others in trouble, you do want to act quickly before things escalate and get out of hand. Think of this as caring for others.

Get support. Confiding in trusted individuals, such as friends, parents, a school counselor, or a therapist can be a great way to talk through the feelings that might be coming up and help soothe any fears or concerns you may be experiencing.

Block communication channels. If cyberbullying is a concern, block and report any unwanted contact with the instigator. You may have to go through all your social media channels and block phone numbers to avoid getting text messages, but it is important to do so. Blocking communication never means you are weak—rather, it means that you are making a wise and prudent decision.

Use the buddy system. Bullies often like to corner whoever their victim is. Consider using the buddy system to walk with friends down the halls, leave class together, and even visit the restroom together. Use your prudence to plan for this. The buddy system can be an added layer of protection for you or a friend in need.

Channel your inner wisdom. Focusing on your inner strengths, such as prudence, social intelligence, curiosity, creativity, humor, and self-regulation, will help you feel empowered and serve as a reminder that you can stick with being uniquely you.

Bullies thrive off of knowing they have an impact on you. Don't give them this satisfaction! Let them see you laughing and smiling. Ignoring them is often the best way of deterring their behavior.

Turn the bully into a frenemy or friend. Clearly it will *not* work in many bullying situations. Consider if you might use your curiosity to learn more about the bully. Sometimes the bully is a lonely, isolated person who does not know how to relate to others. You may be able to have a healthy conversation or even share in an activity. Is there common ground, such as you both like to play basketball or you both enjoy painting or are into the same type of music? You may become the first person to relate to this other person well.

more to do

Depending on how rampant bullying may be at your school, consider taking a bigger leap and getting involved in social justice efforts (your fairness, leadership, and teamwork strengths are at play here). Organizations such as www.stopbullying.gov and www.dosomething.org can help you create support groups at your school that can involve parents and administrators in truly making your school a bully-free zone. Brainstorm a few ways you might be able to do this:

_____

_____

_____

_____

15 are you my friend or frenemy?

Let us be grateful to the people who make us happy; they are the charming gardeners who make our souls blossom.

—Marcel Proust

for you to know

There is no denying that friendships can be complicated. Someone who was your best friend in elementary school may now feel like a sworn enemy, whereas you only met your newest bestie a few short months ago. In many ways, this is the natural course of things as the teen years involve so much growth and identity development. Of course, someone with whom you bonded over cartoons may not be the same person who ends up being just as obsessed with the same pop singer as you!

In an ideal world, you would have no enemies or frenemies. But you also can't control others and their behaviors toward you. You can, however, act from a place of poise, prudence, and peace. You can nurture those friendships that are deeply satisfying and meaningful. In fact, in your busy day, you may have little time for really expressing appreciation to your friends. Outside of birthdays, secret Santas, and other celebrations, it may seem like there are few opportunities for cultivating and maintaining deep friendships and expressing your gratitude. The practice of appreciating their strengths can help you do just this!

for you to do

Pick two of your closest friends and write their names on the top lines of these two columns. Then, for each friend, identify the top three strengths that you have often observed in them and write them under their names (use the list of twenty-four character strengths in the introduction if you need a reminder of these core qualities):

_____   _____

_____   _____

_____   _____

_____   _____

Next, recall a real scenario for each friend in which you witnessed or observed them actively demonstrating one or more of their strengths. It could be when they were using humor during the school play, using bravery to stand up to a bully, or tapping into their spirituality and leadership to organize a vigil. Write what you recall in the space provided.

First friend scenario:

_____

_____

_____

_____

_____

Second friend scenario:

_____

_____

_____

_____

_____

Finally, express your sentiments to your friends! Convey, in your own way, that you appreciate them for their character strengths. This may feel awkward or uncomfortable at first, but it's really not that hard to do. Decide what communication medium feels most comfortable. Maybe you slip a note in their locker, or you send a text acknowledgment. Or take a screenshot of this activity and send it to them!

more to do

There are endless ways of expanding upon this strengths appreciation activity! In fact, the next time Mother's Day or Father's Day comes around, you might consider using this strengths appreciation activity for writing a card to your parent. You can share the strengths you admire and that make you look up to them. If you have been struggling with your relationship with a sibling, you might choose to do this strengths activity with them. Expressing these sentiments can often be the greatest gift we give someone.

16 your key relationship strengths

If you live to be 100, I hope I live to be 100 minus 1 day, so I never have to live without you.

—Winnie the Pooh

for you to know

Studies indicate the most desirable traits a teen friend can have include honesty, humor, kindness, and fairness. This may come as no surprise to you, as most of your friends likely possess these characteristics. While it can be easy to spot (or not!) these traits in others, paying attention to them in yourself may prove to be more challenging.

We are all guilty of being quick to judge others. Someone might be too passive, not friendly enough, too much of a doormat, boring—the list goes on. But how do we pay attention to ourselves and the way we present to the world at large? Being likeable and approachable doesn't have to be about being inauthentic and fake. It really is about taking a look at your own assets and what you bring to the table. That's where your character strengths come into play!

for you to do

Given that there are clearly some key traits related to relationships, consider how you might work on identifying and boosting three of these strengths in yourself. You might even think back to activity 2 and look at the ABC cycle of affect, behavior, and cognitions. Perhaps you will consider cultivating this strength through actively doing something differently in your life, changing your behaviors or changing your thoughts to be more in line with these key strengths. Here are some examples of how to do this.

Curiosity. The next time I have a negative thought (cognitions/thoughts) about a friend or loved one, I will pay attention and become curious about why I am thinking these things. Instead of simply accepting my negative thought as true, I will think about what strengths they have and focus on that instead of any shortcomings I may be focusing on.

Teamwork. During the next basketball playoffs, instead of focusing on my own skills, I will collaborate (behavior/action) with my teammates at a practice session and celebrate (affect/feelings) our hard work together at a pizza party afterward.

Humor. Final exams can be highly stressful for my friends and me. Instead of constantly complaining and absorbing each other's anxious energy, I am going to watch funny YouTube videos daily that make me laugh (affect/feelings) and share them with my friends (behavior/action) to boost our spirits.

Pick any three of the relationship-oriented traits, and write down how you will cultivate these traits in your own life by actively doing something differently.

Honesty: _____

_____

_____

_____

_____

Love: _____

_____

_____

_____

_____

Forgiveness: _____

_____

_____

_____

_____

Kindness: _____

_____

_____

_____

_____

Humility: _____

_____

_____

_____

_____

Fairness: _____

_____

_____

_____

_____

activity 16 ✳ your key relationship strengths

Social intelligence: _____

_____

_____

_____

_____

Zest: _____

_____

_____

_____

_____

more to do

Think of a relationship that may be in need of some extra TLC. Maybe it is a relationship with a girlfriend or a boyfriend or perhaps a parent, best friend, or teacher. We all have relationships that can use some repair, whether due to a hurt or misunderstanding. Think about how you might be able to use any of your strengths to help mend that relationship.

Below, journal about what you could do:

_____

_____

_____

_____

_____

Now see if you might consider taking action. It can often be hard to swallow your pride or ego to take that first step, but it is a sign of humility and courage to do so. Write down how you might take action to mend this relationship. Will you meet this person for coffee? Do you send a note? Come up with the best way to go about taking action, and then do it:

_____

_____

_____

_____

_____

17 stop comparing yourself to others!

Comparison is the thief of joy.

—Theodore Roosevelt

for you to know

Research indicates that frequent social comparisons can have a highly negative impact on your life. Envy, regret, defensiveness, guilt, lying, and blaming others are only some of the behaviors that can result from frequent social comparison.

The theory of social comparison is among the early findings from the pioneering social psychologist Leon Festinger. The theory suggests that humans have an innate need to compare themselves to others and base their sense of self-worth off of this. This comparison can be either positive or negative. For example, you and your friends might compare your physical appearance, academic abilities, athleticism, and other factors to each other and feel better or worse depending on who you are comparing yourself to. If you are a basketball player and compare yourself to someone who is the star player on the team, you might feel more motivated to try harder than ever to do better than them. Or, conversely, you might feel worthless and give up on trying. There are generally three levels of social comparisons:

Upward social comparisons: comparing yourself to someone better off than you (which can result in feeling worse about yourself).

Downward social comparisons: comparing yourself to someone worse off than you (which can result in you feeling better about yourself).

Lateral social comparisons: comparing yourself to someone similarly matched to your own life circumstance and conditions (which can result in neutral feelings overall).

for you to do

If you tend to compare yourself to others, here are some strategies for doing it less often. Place a check mark next to the ones you already do and an X next to the steps you'd like to start practicing:

☐ **Set social media limits.** When you are feeling blue, or even bored, you may jump onto social media without even being consciously aware. If you are already feeling down, looking at everyone living these adventurous lives can make you feel worse about yourself. Consider limiting times you go on social media, or even avoid it altogether during times of the day when you might be more prone to distress.

☐ **Tap your tribe.** It can be common for friends to go from being healthy competitors in a sport to going too far. Consider a way for you and your friends to engage in noncompetitive activities and support each other through positive encouragement and affirmations.

☐ **Focus on the future.** Between endless classes, homework, and exams, no one ever said being a teen was easy. This can lead to negative thought patterns, anxiety, and a sense of being stuck. Instead, fill your locker, room, binder, and notebooks with images, stickers, or other visual representations of the future and of your character strengths.

☐ **Practice gratitude.** Use gratitude lists, journals, or daily prayers to count your blessings and focus on all the great things you do have.

☐ **Remember your character strengths.** In times when it seems that everyone is doing something better than you, go back to your signature strengths that you identified early in this workbook. What were they? How might you tap into them to remember the best parts of yourself when you are feeling down?

more to do

Some of the character strengths that might help you curb social comparisons include not only gratitude but also humility, perspective, judgment/critical thinking, love, forgiveness, and self-regulation. Consider monitoring your urge to compare yourself to others over the next week. Catch yourself when you do. Write down an example of a social comparison that you encountered in any of the categories below:

Upward social comparison: _____

_____

_____

Downward social comparison: _____

_____

_____

Lateral social comparison: _____

_____

_____

Now choose a character strength that you can use to combat comparisons and write about how you will use it. If you get stuck, look back to the survey of character strengths that you completed in the introduction:

_____

_____

_____

getting off (or on) the social media bandwagon 18

Social media has given us this idea that we should all have a posse of friends when in reality, if we have one or two really good friends, we are lucky.

—Brené Brown

for you to know

It might come as no surprise if social media is a normal part of life for you: whether it is the personal thrill of getting a "like" or "love" on social media, or the fact that all of your friends are on it, social media can be tough to escape. When all of your friends are talking about that post that someone just made, it can be easy to feel left out if you aren't on social media. However, you may also be all too familiar with how quickly fights can escalate over social media or how things can be posted in the heat of the moment, screen captured, and memorialized, leading to suspensions or even expulsions. Naturally, social media is a tough beast to defeat.

Having hundreds of followers doesn't necessarily mean you can call them a friend. In fact, how many of them would you really talk to in a time of need? Say you went through a breakup, and you and your friend spent hours talking about it beforehand or discussing the fallout afterward. These personal stories are how we feel close to others, and what distinguish friends from followers. The question, then, is what is really the purpose of social media if they aren't all true friends? Is it for peer validation? To have a venue for flexing and posting images of your glamorous vacations or shopping sprees?

Social media can definitely provide you with some major social benefits, such as a sense of connectedness and a platform to share your creativity and uniqueness. However, there are also times when taking a small step back may be rejuvenative and help you shift your priorities (and time!).

for you to do

Go scroll-free for a week. If you're feeling super brave, try a month! Turn to your character strengths to support you. Perhaps you need to elevate your self-regulation and be disciplined about setting it aside. Maybe you'll turn to kindness and spend the extra time doing something nice for yourself or for others. Or perhaps your creativity will be unleashed: you could try a new hobby and spend time creating something new. You could use your curiosity to explore what it feels like in your body and mind to go without social media for an hour, for a day, and for longer. In 2018, the Royal Society for Public Health out of the United Kingdom came up with a very catchy and approachable way of going scroll-free each September. They suggested five different ways of going scroll-free. Circle the one that meets your needs the most and try it out for a week.

The cold turkey: Giving up all social media accounts for a period of time.

The social butterfly: Not using social media during any social events such as at parties and while dining.

The busy bee: Refraining from social media use during work and school hours.

The night owl: Taking a break from all social media from six p.m. onward.

The sleeping dog: Not using any social media in the bedroom.

Below, record your observations on how your week went. When did staying off social media feel most difficult? When was it the easiest? What helped support you in staying strong and off your devices? Did you have any slipups?

_____

_____

_____

_____

more to do

If you chose one of the easier challenges, such as not using social media in the bedroom, consider picking another one that's harder for you and trying that one for another week. You can do two easier challenges at the same time or do a new harder one on its own. Ideally, you will choose more methods of staying off of social media!

After completing the one-week challenge, you may have come to the realization that certain social media platforms were just not as appealing or exciting any more. Consider deleting that app altogether. If Snapchat is fun and you hardly use Instagram, then get rid of your Instagram accounts. Or if you are someone with a second and third Instagram account, delete your extra accounts.

19 combatting loneliness and isolation

Solitude is not the same as loneliness. Solitude is a solitary boat floating in a sea of possible companions.

—Robert Fulghum

for you to know

What does it mean to be lonely in these 24/7 connected times? When there is always a text coming through, and you are plugged into your devices and surrounded by peers at school and at work, how is it that you can also feel isolated and alone?

According to loneliness expert Kira Asatryan, feeling alone often comes with a sense of lacking closeness with others. Closeness in turn is made up of two key components: *caring* and *knowing*. She describes *caring* as being not just concerned for a friend's struggles but really invested in a friend's overall well-being and showing that your friend matters to you. *Knowing* involves more than just knowledge of facts about someone—it's having a true connection developed over time where you might come to know their likes, dislikes, and even read their mind on occasion!

Many have experienced this common scenario: you are at a party or other social gathering making small talk; you are laughing, nibbling on appetizers, and then you go home feeling utterly empty inside. You were just with people, so what happened? While it may have been an initial boost to be around people, that isn't sufficient for feeling included in a group. The common adage that loneliness is cured by "putting yourself out there" may not work as a means of obtaining closeness.

for you to do

Happiness experts such as Gretchen Rubin believe that loneliness can be a major obstacle to overcome in the path to well-being. Identifying the source of this loneliness can be a key factor in overcoming it. Rubin describes seven forms of loneliness described below. Circle any that apply to you.

1. *New-situation loneliness.* This type of loneliness occurs when you are new to a school, or a new city or other environment.

2. *"I'm different" loneliness.* This type of loneliness occurs when you are in a familiar setting but feel you can't connect with anyone who's similar to you. Maybe you are the only person of color in a predominantly white neighborhood, or the only atheist in a sea of Catholics.

3. *No-sweetheart loneliness.* As it sounds, this is a sense of yearning for a romantic partner. Maybe it is nearing Valentine's day or another holiday, and it feels particularly apparent, or all of your friends are in relationships, and you feel like the third wheel.

4. *No-animal loneliness.* If you have grew up with animals, but your pet died or you're living in an apartment that does not allow animals. As a result, you feel a sense of loneliness without any pet.

5. *No-time-for-me loneliness.* This very common form of loneliness occurs when it feels as like others are too busy for you. Maybe a friend moved away and is too busy with to call, or you have a friend who's making new friends and you feel left out.

6. *Untrustworthy-friends loneliness.* Perhaps you have friends but don't know if you can fully trust them. You don't know if you can be open with them. You may fear your friend will turn on you or talk behind your back, which can make it challenging to be vulnerable.

7. *Quiet-presence loneliness.* Maybe your parents went away for a weekend, or your older brother is off at college. There is a loneliness that comes from missing someone's presence. You may miss a feeling of comfort and stability that you received from their presence even if you weren't always interacting when they were around.

more to do

Once you have identified the types of loneliness that may impact your life, consider making an action plan. While it's impossible to grow instant new friends, you can take an honest look at your existing friends. Who is really there in times of need? What friendships are best to let go of? And which friendships have the potential to blossom into something deeper? Write down your reflections:

_____

_____

_____

_____

_____

See if you can't work on cultivating a greater sense of *caring* and *knowing* with the friends that you have. This doesn't mean you need to have deep hour-long conversations all the time—just a few meaningful face-to-face interactions can do much to increase a sense of closeness. Your character strengths of kindness (doing kind acts), love (being warm and genuine to others), and social intelligence (being empathic and understanding of your friends' feelings) will be very important here. Brainstorm below a few ways you can demonstrate *caring* to your friends:

_____

_____

_____

_____

Finally, brainstorm a few questions you might ask a friend to encourage your depth of *knowing* them. They don't have to be too personal. Just talk about some things that you think might help to bring you closer to one another:

_____

_____

_____

_____

Part 4

Cultivating What Matters Most

Meaning ➜ *Well-Being*

Meaning in life. It sounds like a massive undertaking. But you can think of meaning as finding a sense of purpose and connection in any moment. You can discover meaning by yourself (perhaps walking in nature), with others (feeling connected), or as part of a group or institution (such as volunteering to feed the homeless). The activities in this part of the book, which employ your strengths of gratitude, appreciation of beauty, and social intelligence, will help you transcend what is trivial and mundane to discover those moments of meaning and cultivate what matters most.

20 savor special moments with family

Happy or unhappy, families are all mysterious. We have only to imagine how differently we would be described—and will be, after our deaths—by each of the family members who believe they know us.

—Gloria Steinem

for you to know

To savor something means to prolong the positive. When you eat a piece of chocolate as slowly as you can, relishing the richness and the flavor, you are actually practicing savoring. You can also savor your relationships. Think of a happy conversation you had with your mother. Reflect on a family vacation to the beach. Think of the time when you and a sibling were laughing uncontrollably. For any of these experiences, if you allow yourself to reexperience the positive feelings, allowing them to linger, then you are practicing savoring.

Savoring is a great practice if you are looking for a well-being boost. While research shows it can give you a shot of happiness, part of what happens when you savor past memories is you are tapping into your sense of nostalgia. This is important for experiencing greater meaning in your life.

for you to do

Let's bring some specific steps to savoring with an activity commonly referred to as *positive reminiscence.* This involves savoring a positive memory. For this activity, let's target your family.

1. Bring to mind a pleasant memory you had with one of your family members (or with your family together as a group).

2. Replay the pleasant memory as a story in your mind where you can see and hear the details and you can feel the positivity as you reflect.

3. Use your character strengths to intensify the positive feelings of the memory. For example, use your curiosity to explore the details, creativity to visualize the positive memory from different perspectives, and love and gratitude to experience positive emotions in the moment now as you reflect.

4. Journal about your experience and your thoughts on these questions: What stood out most to you in your positive reminiscence? What is it like to *savor* a relationship? What are the elements that made that experience with family strong? What character strengths did you see in your family members?

5. Consider sharing this memory and savoring activity with one or more of your family members.

more to do

Savoring can be directed to enjoying the present or to imagining the future, appreciating other relationships, and relishing your own strengths!

Savor your present. Go somewhere you enjoy inside or just outside your home. You might go near a babbling brook or on top of a hill, or you might go to a quiet place in your basement or room. Use your senses to savor your environment in the present moment. Soak up the uniqueness of what you see, hear, smell, and touch. Allow yourself to feel the positive emotions that emerge and flow within you for at least ten minutes.

Savor your future. Isn't it great to anticipate a fun event or a gathering coming up that you are excited about? Perhaps you'll be going on a new date, attending a sporting event, or going on a family trip. Take advantage of this upcoming positive experience by deliberately savoring it. Rather than randomly daydreaming about it, sit down and reflect on the potential details and the positive feelings you might experience during it.

Savor with others. The next time you are with a friend or family member, bring up a shared positive event you had with them. Recall the details together. Be open to the laughter, joy, and grateful feelings that may arise as you connect with this person about your shared memory.

Savor a strength. After completing one of the savoring activities you've just read about, name a character strength that you used in the experience. Perhaps it was gratitude that you felt for another person, appreciation of beauty while out in nature, or perseverance as you stuck with the savoring activity for additional time? Pause to savor this positive strength and the positive feelings that go with it.

build an attitude of 21 gratitude

Gratitude is the healthiest of all human emotions. The more you express gratitude for what you have, the more likely you will have even more to express gratitude for.

—Zig Ziglar

for you to know

Gratitude is one of the easiest strengths to build. But, like any practice in this book, it takes repetition and practice over time. Gratitude can be seen in your saying "thank you" when someone does something nice for you or in your extension of appreciation to someone for inviting you to a party or event. But your gratitude has the potential to go much deeper. You can sit down with a friend or a family member and share how important they are to you and how much you value them. This deeper approach to gratitude builds relationships and forges long-term connections with others. It helps you as well as others feel good. It is in this way that gratitude can be a gift you offer to someone.

The practice of gratitude has a number of benefits, as discovered in scientific studies over the last fifteen to twenty years. These include better physical and psychological health, more meaning in life, better grades in school, and greater goal achievement. In addition, gratitude is one of five strengths that is most linked with happiness. If you are feeling down or dejected or lost in self-pity or isolation, you might be able to lift yourself out of it by doing something that seems counterintuitive to your feelings—to turn to being grateful. Grateful for what? Grateful for your life, grateful for the people in it, grateful for your autonomy to take action and make changes for the better, and so on.

for you to do

Let's try a popular activity that has been shown to boost happiness and decrease depression. It's called counting the good or counting your blessings. Here are the steps of this classic gratitude-building strategy:

1. At the end of the day, reflect on what went well.

2. In a digital or paper journal, write down three things that went well during the day *and* why you think they went well. Be specific. For example, rather than saying "I'm grateful for my family," say "I'm grateful that my mom and I talked about my trouble with Joanie today." Rather than saying "I'm grateful for my health," consider saying "I'm grateful for the zestful energy I felt during the twenty-minute walk I took this morning."

3. Do this practice for one week, but consider doing it for longer.

To get the most out of this exercise, we suggest you never repeat the same thing twice. Really look at your day to find even very small things to be grateful for, such as when someone held the door for you, when you exchanged a smile with a classmate, or when you learned you'd be arriving home fifteen minutes early. This laser focus on the good things will help you expand your strength of gratitude, making it a stronger part of who you are. Imagine if you did this activity each day for one year—you would end up with over a thousand unique expressions of gratitude!

more to do

Be grateful for you! Gratitude is typically referred to as being *other oriented* because you are focusing your attention on the other person with your gratitude. But gratitude can also be directed inward. Reflect on your most core qualities—your character strengths that make up what is best in you. Extend gratitude to these strengths by reflecting on why you value these strengths, how they help you, how they benefit others, and why you like yourself for these strengths.

You can also write a gratitude letter. Think of one or more people in your life—living or deceased—whom you have not properly thanked for the positive impact they have had upon you. Write a letter to them explaining how important they have been to you. You do not have to share the letter. Remember, this is really about recognizing the role others have had in your life and appreciating them by writing down your grateful thoughts.

22 create mindfulness moments of strength

To live is the rarest thing in the world. Most people exist, that is all.

—Oscar Wilde

for you to know

"Live in the moment." "Look within." "Take it one moment at a time." "Face your problems directly." "Just stop and breathe." "Be in the here-and-now." No doubt you've heard these phrases before. Each of these maxims is attempting to capture the essence of mindfulness. You've probably heard that mindfulness is a form of meditation, but it's actually much more. Mindfulness means taking control of your attention rather than staying lost in mind wandering, distraction, and daydreaming.

All of us have minds that wander. A lot. Your mind wanders when you're driving as you think about your upcoming day, it wanders while you're eating as you recall a conversation with a friend, and it wanders when you're talking to others as you think about where you're going next. This is all entirely normal. Your autopilot mind is hardwired into you, and while you cannot get rid of it, you can notice its content and where it goes. In many ways, your autopilot mind helps you to take a mental break, to solve problems, and to build creativity. When your autopilot mind is running too much of your life, however, things can become problematic.

for you to do

A simple yet empowering tool that you can use at any time is called *the mindful pause*. This is a quick way to short-circuit your autopilot mind wandering, become connected into the present moment, and shift your mindset to mindfulness and character strengths. Consider these three easy steps that you can use at any point during your day:

1. Pause and feel your in-breath and out-breath for fifteen seconds. Let everything go except for your breathing. Give your breath your full attention.

2. Conclude with a question: *Which of my character strengths might I bring forward right now?*

3. Take notice of the strength that emerges for you as a word, image, sound, story, or idea. Take positive action with this strength.

Try out this breathing activity now! Then, build upon what you learn from it about your character strengths. This exercise is about trusting yourself and the natural wisdom and strengths within you. Remember you have twenty-four character strengths that you can use as resources, so be open to your full self. Whatever comes up, go with it! Your thoughts, like yourself, are unique to you.

more to do

There are many pathways to creating greater mindfulness in your life. Here are some useful tips for bringing mindfulness into daily routines, special events, or other activities in your life.

Return to your senses. When you attend to one or more of your five senses, you are practicing mindfulness in the present moment. You are more tuned in to your internal perceptions, sensations, thoughts, and feelings, even when they are unpleasant or painful. To practice this mindfulness skill of observing what is going on, bring forth your curiosity to notice the sensations in your body and your thoughts and feelings about whatever you are doing.

Eliminate multitasking. Much of life involves doing many things at once. You've probably become so good at this that sometimes you don't even recognize when you are multitasking (reading a text while walking, watching television while eating, talking to someone while posting on social media, and so on). This tip involves trying to do one thing at a time whenever possible.

Slow down. With whatever you are doing, can you do it slower? Walk at half your typical speed, put your fork or spoon down between bites, or drive five miles per hour slower. Take notice of how this opens up your mindfulness.

Describe your way to mindfulness. Describing is a core skill of mindfulness, and it means labeling and detailing the facts and truth of the situation. It also means being able to notice and label in words your beliefs, opinions, emotions, and expectations, which may be different from the facts of the situation! To get perspective, try stepping back from any situation by describing it to yourself. Mindfulness is about seeing things clearly and honestly, so this skill of describing involves your use of social intelligence, bravery, and perspective to see the details of the situation and the bigger picture.

mindful walking in nature 23

In every walk with nature one receives far more than he seeks.

—John Muir

for you to know

Shinrin-yoku is the Japanese term used to describe forest bathing. Developed in the 1980s, it refers to peaceful, deeply healing, and preventative health practices that involve meditative walks under a forest canopy. While there are some specialized therapy programs that involve particular meditations or procedures, the important elements are bringing your awareness to your senses in the present moment and being in the natural environment, breathing fresh air, slowing down, and letting your mind refocus. Several groups of researchers across the globe have found that mindful walking in nature can bring a host of benefits including:

- Increases in positive emotions

- Decreases in blood pressure

- Decreases in stress

- Increases in immune functioning

- Increases in focus

- Increases in energy

- Improved sleep

Not bad at all for time spent communing with nature! Of course, our busy lives can prevent us from taking such time for contemplation and intentionality. However, making the time even once a month (weather permitting!) to visit a forest and spend some time there can be deeply healing.

for you to do

Go on a forest walk! While it is helpful to find someplace relatively peaceful and quiet, it is important to ensure your safety, so you might consider bringing along a parent or a friend. Our example will focus on being outdoors in the woods, but if that is not easily accessible for you, and you want to take action right now, then simply go outside in your neighborhood; practice experiencing your neighborhood with what mindfulness teachers refer to as a *beginner's mind,* where you see, listen, and walk around your neighborhood with fresh eyes and ears, experiencing it as if for the first time. During your walk, consider using the following guide to help you focus on your sensations and escape the constant stream of thoughts you might typically experience.

Sight: Observe all the minutiae of your surroundings from the tiniest twigs to large, powerful trunks of trees that have been there for over a century.

Sounds: Listen for every crackle of twigs breaking and crunching of leaves. Listen for the sounds of the wind sweeping through the trees. Birds may chirp, squirrels may chase each other. Hear the forest's unique symphony.

Smells: Take in the woodsy scent, the smell of pine, cedar, or whatever type of foliage you are experiencing. Olfactory memories can be so powerful, so make some new ones at the forest.

Touch: As you walk, allow your fingers to graze gently past the leaves on branches or lightly touch tree trunks. Feel the rough ridges and the soft moss. Ground down through your feet and feel the undulations of the forest trails and path, each foot stepping ahead of the other, supported by nature.

Taste: Take many slow deep breaths, filling your lungs and body with the cleansing air.

As you walk, use your strengths. Will you walk slowly and carefully with your strength of prudence or with energy and vigor using your zest? Will you marvel in awe and appreciation of beauty as you take in the novelty of nature? What will you be most curious about? What will most pique your love of learning? These and many other character strengths will be ready for you to use in the experience.

more to do

Bring nature into your home! There are many ways of re-creating the experience of being in nature. Perhaps you buy a few small indoor plants and keep them watered regularly. You might notice that each time you water the soil, you get the distinct aroma of nature (and lawn care stores!). You might light a scented candle that has a woodsy scent to it or listen to nature sounds. There are many creative ways to bring the soothing calm of nature into your everyday life. Below, list some ideas for some ways you might bring nature into your life using the five senses:

Sight: _____

_____

Sound: _____

_____

Smell: _____

_____

Touch: _____

_____

Taste: _____

_____

Everything has beauty, but not everyone sees it.

—Confucius

for you to know

Awe and elevation are two related emotions that you don't want to live without. These two emotions within you involve your response to beauty or to goodness in the world. Awe occurs when you are struck by the intense colors of a sunset over a lake or ocean, the expansive vastness of the night sky, or by stunning nature pictures on Instagram. Awe can trigger additional positive feelings and decrease anxiety while giving you a wider sense of perspective.

Elevation is an emotion you feel when you observe goodness or moral beauty, such as when you see others use their character strengths of kindness, bravery, forgiveness, or fairness to help others. You might see a friend courageously confront a bully, your parent kindly attending to your sick brother or sister, or a character in a movie display compassion and forgiveness to an enemy. With a sense of elevation, after observing this moral goodness, you may feel a warming in your chest or tingling in your hands or in your arms. And then, and most importantly, you are motivated to do good as well. Research shows that elevation often leads to more acts of kindness to others.

for you to do

Awe and elevation are uplifting, feel-good emotions. Why not try to create more situations in your life where you can experience them? One way is to be strategic about the media (movies, television, social media, and music) that you take in.

1. Select a form of media that you'd like to focus on and that has a good likelihood of generating feelings of awe or elevation. Examples you might select include movies, television series, or photo-driven social media such as Instagram.

2. In whatever media you've selected, investigate where you can most easily find or watch inspiring material. Perhaps you'll search for an inspiring movie about courage, a television series about the natural world, or search platforms for photographers who capture beauty in nature or in the human experience.

3. Save, follow, friend, star, or add to your list those people or shows that are likely to inspire awe or elevation.

4. Make a plan to spend time with this awe-inducing or elevating material once or twice a week.

more to do

Awe and elevation are outgrowths of your appreciation of beauty and excellence. You can develop this character strength in a number of ways that have been discussed in research studies. Here are some suggestions:

Write about three beautiful things that you noticed today. Did you notice beauty in the natural environment, in art or music, or in the kind actions of others? As you think about these three beautiful things, write about how they occurred and any circumstances that brought you to take notice of each. Try noticing three beautiful things as a daily practice.

Create a beauty portfolio. Create an online portfolio, such as on Instagram, of beauty that you see in the world that fills you with awe or elevation. Share it with others. If you prefer a nondigital approach, then create a scrapbook.

Add beauty to your environment. Enhance your home, room, locker, or workspace by deliberately bringing more beauty and inspiration into it. This might include plants, photographs, or objects that mean something special to you.

25 cultivating spirituality and the sacred

Just to be is a blessing. Just to live is holy.

—Abraham Joshua Heschel

for you to know

Spirituality can be boiled down to one word: sacred. Large numbers of scientists now define spirituality as the search for, or connecting with, the sacred. That which is sacred or holy or blessed or precious can be different for each person. Common examples of the sacred include nature, God, a higher power, all of life (sentient beings), our collective consciousness, or deep meaning. On a personal level, this connection might be described as your feeling of wonder, awe, compassion, inner peace, gratitude, hope, amazement, purpose, or interconnection with others.

This personal view of spirituality can be distinguished from being religious. That is, it is different from following prescribed beliefs—engaging in certain faith rituals or activities with others—that are offered by a religious group or institution. Religiousness can be a pathway to deepening spirituality, but it isn't the only way.

The affiliation referred to as *spiritual but not religious* has been one of the fastest growing groups in the United States for nearly two decades and is especially common among young people. A 2017 survey from the Pew Research Center found that 29 percent of people under age thirty describe themselves this way. The most common spiritually meaningful practices that people report include activities with family, friends, food, and pets. Additional spiritual practices people commonly report include prayer, time in nature, music, art, sports, yoga, meditation, hiking, travel, and journaling.

for you to do

Your spiritual self and your spiritual life is unique to you. It is not something for anyone else to tell you what it should or should not be like. This activity is designed to help you ponder, grapple with, discover, and make sense of your own spirituality. We encourage you to journal about your reflections and insights with each step.

1. First, explore: What matters most to you, or what is most meaningful for you in your life? What does spirituality mean to you? Do you think there is a deeper purpose in the universe? Do you have a fulfilling way of expressing your spirituality, such as through a ritual, a practice, or participation in a community? What helps you connect with the sacred in your life?

2. Getting more specific, can you name a situation in which you felt a strong sense of meaning or a distinct sense of connection with the sacred in your life, whether it be one time, ten times, or a hundred times? It could be an awe-inspiring sunset, a profound experience during meditation or a religious service, a special conversation with someone at work or in your class, volunteering at a local nonprofit, or receiving kindness from a stranger. Those are just a few ideas to jump-start your reflection.

3. Build on your experience. While you cannot necessarily re-create the situation in which you felt a strong sense of spirituality, perhaps you can put yourself in a position to have more of those moments? Using the examples just mentioned, you could make sure you see one sunset every week, practice meditation daily, have coffee again with the person you connected with, volunteer more regularly, or engage in your own random acts of kindness.

4. Take action. What step forward might you take?

more to do

Take a *technology fast*. This is a good way to cut back on the noise and activity of everyday life that can distract us from connecting with things that we find sacred. Try a technology fast where, for a period of time, you set aside (or hide from yourself!) your smart-phone and computer and you keep all external noise to a minimum (or turned off), such as televisions, chatting or emailing, and car radio or music. Try this out for one day, probably a weekend where you don't have much schoolwork to do. If that seems too difficult, you can also start smaller by choosing a specified amount of time to fast, such as three hours away from technology distractions. Take notice of how you feel during and after the fast. Journal how you felt before and afterward.

Here are some other things you can do to develop your spirituality.

Use your other strengths as pathways. Research shows that the character strengths most likely to co-occur with the strength of spirituality are gratitude, hope, zest, love, and kindness. Might one of these five strengths offer you another pathway for tapping into your spirituality? Could you deliberately practice being more grateful or kind? More loving in one of your relationships? More zestful and hopeful when you are with others at school?

Rediscover silence. Go into a quiet space, indoors or out. Take notice of the sound of silence. How does it feel? Use your strength of bravery to face any anxiety you may have about sitting in the quiet. When you are in silence, take time to listen to yourself. What do you hear? What needs, feelings, or insights do you notice? Some spiritual teachers explain this is listening to "that still, small voice" inside. See if you can discover yours.

Learn from a spiritual role model. Think of someone in your life who is particularly kind, forgiving, fair-minded, gentle, humble, or grateful. What do you appreciate most about this person? What is at least one positive attribute you would like to emulate? What might you do to take one positive step forward in acting in that way?

overcoming jealousy, envy, and FOMO 26

Envy is pain at the good fortune of others.

—Aristotle

for you to know

In today's ever status-conscious world, it seems everyone you know is broadcasting their latest gadget, vacation, or other good fortune. There is a reason, after all, that the term *Facebook depression* was coined in the new millennium. When witnessing everyone else living their best life or at least pretending to, your own life may seem mundane and uninspired. This need not be the case, though, when you start integrating healthy doses of gratitude, awe, laughter, and joy into your daily experience.

The notion of *fear of missing out* (FOMO) can lead many teens to run themselves ragged. If this sounds like you, perhaps your weekend is a back-to-back series of sports games, parties, and other events. You almost never turn down an invitation. You are so busy squeezing out every last bit of possible joy and engagement in your life that you wind up burned out and exhausted. After that, you may start to feel a bit depressed or even resentful of others who appear to be able to juggle so many balls at once.

Life needn't become a delicate balancing act between overdoing it or succumbing to jealousy or envy at what everyone else is doing. Through reprioritizing your time commitments and focusing on your own well-being, you can start paying attention to what really matters to you—and not what will make you a more popular person or what looks good on college applications. In fact, trying to be who others want you to be rather than who you want to be is a surefire path to unhappiness and discontent. Focusing on your values instead can be the strongest and wisest path forward.

for you to do

Below are six virtues that are valued and present across beliefs, religions, and cultures. No doubt you value many (or all) of these in your life too! Check off the two virtues that stand out to you the most. They can be whatever resonates the most with you:

☐ Wisdom (knowledge strengths)

☐ Courage (adversity strengths)

☐ Humanity (interpersonal strengths)

☐ Justice (community strengths)

☐ Temperance (protective strengths)

☐ Transcendence (meaning strengths)

Now, think about how these virtues may align with values that you hold dear. For example, you could value intelligence, ambition, peace, family, spirituality, adventure, or beauty. (You may want to look online for a list of values for further inspiration!) Write down your top two virtues, and underneath, list any of your values that align with those virtues.

Virtue 1: _____

Values that align with this virtue: _____

_____

_____

_____

Virtue 2: _____

Values that align with this virtue: _____

_____

_____

_____

Next, consider how you might shift your current commitments to create more space for manifesting your virtues. You can do this by prioritizing and expressing what you value. For example, if you really value time with family but are never around to spend time with them, you might consider instigating a family movie and board-game night. Brainstorm some strategies for prioritizing what you value (and manifesting your virtues):

Virtue 1: _____

Strategies for prioritizing values: _____

_____

_____

_____

Virtue 2: _____

Strategies for prioritizing values: _____

_____

_____

_____

Enact some of your strategies for prioritizing your values. Finally, reflect on how doing this has changed your emotional temperature. Are you feeling less stressed? More connected? Less resentful?

_____

_____

_____

_____

more to do

Jealously-proof your life! In addition to living a life more in line with your values, consider the following additional tips to avoid FOMO and live your best life:

- ☑ **Avoid comparisons!** Review activity 17 on upward and downward social comparisons.

- ☑ **Don't let social media get you down.** Review activity 18 for setting healthy limits on your device usage.

- ☑ **Boost your self-esteem.** Turn to part 5 to start learning more. You will feel more confident and self-assured than ever before!

- ☑ **Surround yourself with true friends.** Review activity 15 for making friends versus frenemies.

Part 5

Your Goals, Your Life

Accomplishment → Well-Being

You have already achieved many things in your life and accomplished some of your goals. No doubt you have used a growth mindset at times where you see setbacks and failures as opportunities to learn from. And, your strengths of perseverance to overcome obstacles, perspective to see the bigger picture of your direction in life, and the energy of your zest strength each play an important role. The activities in this section will offer you more steps and strategies to stay on the path of feeling effective and being effective.

27 your best possible self

The future belongs to those who believe in the beauty of their dreams.

—Eleanor Roosevelt

for you to know

You are probably already using your imagination a lot, and not just when you are daydreaming or fantasizing. You may imagine scenarios that might happen to you at work or at school, imagine what friends will say when you arrive with your new outfit, or imagine the responses and emojis and likes you'll receive to your recent post. And you may often imagine what you'd like to do over the upcoming weekend. You can also use your imagination to boost your well-being.

This activity will invite you to look into your future and envision yourself in a way that is pleasing and empowering for you. Using your imagination in this way can give you greater hope and optimism, help you manage problems or stressors, and improve your mood. For many people, it's an important activity for clarifying and eventually reaching their goals. Different versions of this activity have been shown to bring benefit to a wide range of people, from children to adults, including those suffering with depression or anxiety symptoms.

for you to do

Do the following to make the most of this popular and powerful activity.

1. **Close your eyes and imagine.** Take a few minutes to think about your life in the future, about one year from now. Imagine that everything has gone well for you. You have worked hard and accomplished many goals. Think of this as reaching your full potential, hitting an important milestone, or realizing one of your life dreams. Reach high and also be realistic.

2. **Gather the details.** Now visualize the details of your life in this scenario of your best possible self in a year. Gather as many details as you can. Be open to different possibilities, some of which may surprise you, others you might expect.

3. **Get it on paper.** As the image and details become clear to you, write down what you've imagined. The exercise of writing this down helps to build clarity and understanding, and it helps you link your thoughts and ideas together.

4. **Find your strengths.** Review what you have written and ask yourself: *Which character strengths (of the twenty-four) are apparent in what I wrote down? And which character strengths will be most important for me to use to make this vision a reality?*

5. **Take action.** What is one small thing you might do today to take action toward your best possible self?

more to do

There are different ways you can do this activity, improve it, or tailor it more closely to your preferences and needs.

Get more specific. Rather than focusing on your life in general, you might like to focus on one particular domain of your life, such as "your best possible self in a relationship" or "your best possible self at work."

Handle your problems. Choose something you are struggling with. If you are having difficulty making friends or are feeling lonely or isolated, then consider focusing this activity as "your best possible self with friends." If you are upset about your relationship with one of your parents, then consider "your best possible self as a son or daughter." Go through the steps with this new focus.

Change the time parameters. Rather than one year, consider the time frame in a more immediate way, such as one month from now. This can be useful for setting and reaching short-term goals. Alternatively, you can take the longer view and imagine your best possible self later in your life, such as five years from now.

Tap into a wide range of strengths. For step 4, get more specific about your strengths and investigate each of your specific signature strengths as a unique pathway to your best possible self. How might you use your number one signature strength to reach your best possible self? Your number two signature strength? And so on. You might also consider other character strengths that are particularly important for goal setting, such as hope, perseverance, and prudence. How might tapping into these strengths further support you?

We are all in the gutter, but some of us are looking at the stars.

—Oscar Wilde

for you to know

Your strength of hope goes hand in glove with your life goals. Hope means having positive expectations about the future, while your life goals are what you strive toward. Building hope for your goals involves two learnable skills that researchers have found to be key:

Pathways thinking. You perceive that you can create goals and follow any of multiple ways to reach them.

Agency thinking. You perceive that you can keep up the energy and motivation to follow through with your goals.

for you to do

Try out these two skills for yourself with a specific goal!

1. Name your goal, or one thing you'd like to accomplish, such as a getting a new job, building up your bravery, asking someone out on a date, or improving your grade point average. Write your goal here:

   _____

2. Use pathways thinking. Create many pathways to achieve your goal. Write down at least three different possible path that could help you accomplish your goal. Which character strengths will help you get there?

   _____

   _____

3. Use agency thinking. Build in thoughts to increase your confidence in reaching toward your goals. For example, *I can take this one step at a time; I've taken similar steps like this before; My signature strengths give me confidence that I can do it;* or *I want to challenge myself in this way.*

   _____

   _____

more to do

Keep a growth mindset. This means seeing your failures, your setbacks, and your struggles as opportunities for growth. You can learn a lot from your failures. Failure can help you build new knowledge and ideas and do better the next time. Meeting new challenges will help you grow and be more successful. Is the teacher who doesn't believe in you an opportunity for you to prove yourself? Might getting rejected by someone be a chance to meet new people and broaden yourself? Is not getting on the sports team or into the college of your choice an opportunity to work even harder or pursue unexpected and exciting avenues?

Name a time when you were rejected or experienced a setback or failure.

_____

_____

What did you learn from this experience?

_____

_____

What character strengths could you bring forward in the future to respond differently to a similar experience?

_____

_____

29 taming your inner critic

Feeling compassion for ourselves in no way releases us from responsibility for our actions. Rather, it releases us from the self-hatred that prevents us from responding to our life with clarity and balance.

—Tara Brach

for you to know

Chances are you don't have to look far to find your toughest critic—it's you! Self-criticism that is constructive, fair, and thoughtful can be motivating and help you achieve many things in life. That's important to remember as you simultaneously cultivate self-compassion and balanced thinking.

It is easy to go too far, so your inner critic becomes a judge who looks for any flaw or misstep and levels you with harsh meanness that makes your mistake, error, or failure much worse. Fortunately, you can cultivate self-compassion, loving-kindness, and resilience, which research has shown can benefit your well-being and stress.

for you to do

Start with an ancient (and now modern day) practice called *metta,* or loving-kindness, meditation. This involves directing mindful attention toward the character strength of love that resides within you. Practice with these steps a few times this week:

1. Find a quiet place where you can be alone and reflect.

2. Think of someone in your life whom you have felt deeply loved by. Reflect on a specific situation in which you were fully and genuinely loved by that person.

3. Allow yourself to feel the love from that person in that situation as if it were happening right now. Open yourself to notice the feelings and sensations of love in your body.

4. Then recite the following four lines of meditation (which originated thousands of years ago!) a few times to yourself.

    May I be filled with loving-kindness,

    May I be safe from inner and outer dangers,

    May I be well in body and mind,

    May I be at ease and happy.

As you say each line to yourself, try coming up with an image for the words. Pause after each line and allow yourself to dwell in the positive feelings that arise.

more to do

After cultivating your inner strength of love from practicing this loving-kindness meditation for at least a week, reflect on the questions that follow. As you answer them, you will gain greater insight into actions you can take to bounce back from harsh self-criticism.

1. **Talk back.** Challenge your inner critic. It's okay to disagree. Using your bravery and perseverance strengths, what might you say back when your inner critic appears too intense?

    _____

    _____

2. **Find balance.** Find your strengths of fairness and forgiveness. When your inner critic is particularly strong, ask yourself, *What is a fair way for me to think about this? What would I say to a friend with a similar problem with their inner critic? Might I forgive myself for any mistake I've made, for being imperfect? Is there some tension I might let go of relating to my error?*

    _____

    _____

3. **Be gentle.** Slowing down and softening your intensity helps you change the way that you relate to yourself. Have your relationship with yourself be a gentle one. What might be a gentle or kind thing you say to yourself when your inner judge is taking things too far?

    _____

    _____

4. **Remember your uniqueness.** You are irreplaceable and capable of making an important contribution in this world. Explore how this is true. Which of your character strengths might help you most in using your uniqueness to contribute to the world?

_____

_____

5. **Pursue growth.** How might you learn from your inner critic? Setting aside anything harsh or mean, what is the underlying message that might help you grow?

_____

_____

6. **Uncover your resilience.** How have you bounced back when you were down or stuck in negative thinking in the past?

_____

_____

7. **Keep perspective.** What matters most to you? What people do you matter most to? What character strengths do they see in you?

_____

_____

When times are tough, it's helpful to remind yourself of the answers to these questions.

Part 6

Healthy Body, Healthy Mind

Your Positive Health → Well-Being

One of the quickest ways to feel better and build your sense of well-being is to take positive action to improve your health. This takes the discipline of self-regulation, some planning with prudence, and the energy of perseverance. You can start by taking one small step toward greater health today, and the activity that follows will show you how.

30 promoting good health

To keep the body in good health is a duty...otherwise we shall not be able to keep our mind strong and clear.

—Siddhartha Gautama (the Buddha)

for you to know

One of the most important ways to boost your well-being is by improving your physical health. Scores of research show that you can improve our health (even if you have a chronic illness) by building in a healthy lifestyle. There are five main pillars of good health that we invite you to activate to feel alive and vital, strong in body and mind! These are illustrated in the figure 3.

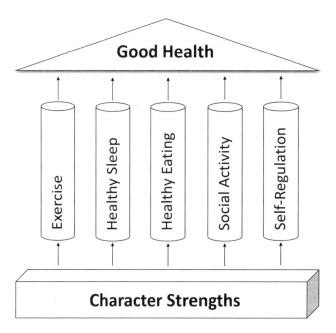

Figure 3: Five Pillars of Good Health

Figure from Ryan Niemiec's *The Strengths-Based Workbook for Stress Relief.*

Here's how the five pillars support good health:

1. **Exercise or movement:** following an exercise plan or a schedule for regular movement or walking to increase your activity and bodily motion, like steps taken per day.

2. **Sleep:** getting quality, uninterrupted sleep daily, usually seven to nine hours per night, to feel generally refreshed upon awakening.

3. **Eating and drinking:** consuming a healthy diet high in fruits and vegetables, along with other essential nutrients and plenty of daily water, and managing the intake of unhealthy foods, such as foods with high sugars, trans fat, carbs, fast food, alcohol, and drugs.

4. **Social activity:** having a regular outlet for your social life with friends, family, and community, such as volunteering and engaging in a spiritual group, to enrich your life meaning.

5. **Self-regulation practice:** engaging in a regular practice of calming, centering, or strengths boosting to take care of and regulate yourself (examples include relaxation strategies, mindfulness, prayer, time in silence, and loving-kindness meditation).

for you to do

Which of the five pillars of health is already strong for you? Maybe you go to bed at the same time each night or eat several servings of fruit each day. Maybe it's part of your routine to connect with friends each week by phone or during outings. It's likely you are particularly strong in one or more of the five pillars. Write down the area that's going well and answer the questions that follow.

Area that's going well: _____

What are you doing to make that area successful for your health?

_____

_____

Now, recall your five signature strengths. How have you used one or more of your signature strengths to help you keep up with this health habit?

_____

_____

Now pick an area that you'd like to work on. Write it down and answer the questions that follow.

Area that needs your attention: _____

Why did you choose this area? What is motivating you to attend to it?

_____

_____

Look again to your signature strengths, your natural sources of energy and motivation. How might you use one of your signature strengths to help you improve in this health area?

_____

_____

more to do

Just like you might receive a prescription of medicine to help your headache, chronic depression, or back pain, try giving yourself a prescription for better health. This activity will help you create the perfect behavioral prescription for your health.

Remember that the journey toward better health starts with just one step! Review the five pillars and what you've reflected on so far in this activity, and consider the next question. What is one step you'd be willing to take this week for your health? What signature strength will help you take this action?

Here's an example:

Health area: Sleep

Plan: I will go to bed by 9:00 p.m. each day and will do a relaxing breathing activity starting at 8:45 p.m. to slow myself down.

Signature strength: Prudence

How you'll use it: Prudence will help me start my bedtime preparations by 8:30 p.m. and help me make time to do a calming exercise right before sleep.

Now come up with your own prescription. What health area (pillar) will you focus on? What plan of action will you take this week? Remember no action is too small! What signature strength will you rely on, and how will you use it? Fill in the blanks for your personal prescription:

Health area: _____

Plan: _____

_____

_____

Signature strength: _____

How you'll use it: _____

_____

_____

_____

conclusion

Congratulations on making it through this workbook! Hopefully it has equipped you with the tools and skills you need to start truly living your fullest, most zestful life possible. While it may seem like a luxury at times to focus on yourself and your well-being, the truth is that it is essential. Without focusing on yourself, it can be nearly impossible to attend to the countless things that demand your time and attention.

Throughout this book, you have learned some key elements for boosting your happiness and building up your emotional resiliency. Through learning how to identify emotions (activity 1) and manage them when they become stressful (activity 7), you've learned to be in charge of your emotions instead of letting them run your life. In so doing, you've engaged with the opportunities that await you by tapping into your motivation (activity 8) and cultivating your best possible self (activity 27).

Meanwhile, focusing on healthy relationships (activities 15 and 16) propelled you forward, knowing that you have a tribe that is cheering you on in your endeavors! If you have sometimes felt bored (activity 13) and uninspired, you have learned some invaluable insights on living an inspired life full of awe (activity 24) and gratitude (activity 21). These are all skills that will ultimately help you in your future endeavors, no matter how great your ambitions and goals may be!

We are so honored that you allowed us into your lives during the incredible journey of your teenage years. May you carry forward the joy and energy of these years into every stage of your life, and may wisdom guide you throughout all of your days.

further reading

The Power of Character Strengths: Appreciate and Ignite Your Positive Personality (by Ryan Niemiec and Robert McGrath)

The Social Media Workbook for Teens: Skills to Help You Balance Screen Time, Manage Stress, and Take Charge of Your Life (by Goali Saedi Bocci)

The Strengths-Based Workbook for Stress Relief: A Character Strengths Approach to Finding Calm in the Chaos of Daily Life (by Ryan Niemiec)

Digital Detox Card Deck: 56 Practices to Help You Detox, De-Stress, Distract, and Discover (by Goali Saedi Bocci)

Flourish: A Visionary New Understanding of Happiness and Well-Being (by Martin Seligman)

references

Introduction

Niemiec, R. M. 2018. *Character Strengths Interventions: A Field Guide for Practitioners*. Boston: Hogrefe.

Peterson, C., and M. E. P. Seligman. 2004. *Character Strengths and Virtues: A Handbook and Classification*. New York: Oxford University Press, and Washington, DC: American Psychological Association.

Seligman, M. E. P. 2011. *Flourish: A Visionary New Understanding of Happiness and Well-Being*. New York: Free Press.

Part 1. Manifesting Positive Vibes

Activity 1. Identifying Positive Emotions

Fredrickson, B. 2001. "The Role of Positive Emotions in Positive Psychology: The Broaden and Build Theory of Positive Emotions." *American Psychologist* 56 (3): 218–26.

Activity 2. The ABCs of Mood

McLeod, S. A. 2019. "Cognitive Behavioral Therapy." January 11. https://www.simplypsychology.org/cognitive-therapy.html.

Activity 3. Forecasting Your Mood

Gilbert, D. T. 2007. *Stumbling on Happiness*. New York: Vintage.

Activity 4. Happiness (Zest Booster!)

Diener, E., R. A. Emmons, R. J. Larsen, and S. Griffin. 1985. "The Satisfaction with Life Scale." *Journal of Personality Assessment* 49: 71–75.

Activity 5. Optimism (Hope Booster!)

Wadey, K. 2010. "Explanatory Style: Methods of Measurement and Research Findings." March 2. http://positivepsychology.org.uk/explanatory-style/.

Activity 6. LOL and Live Fully (Humor Booster!)

Louie, D., K. Brook, and E. Frates. 2016. "The Laughter Prescription: A Tool for Lifestyle Medicine." *American Journal of Lifestyle Medicine* 10 (4): 262–67.

Activity 7. How Positive Emotions Can Relieve Mental Stress

Park, N., and C. Peterson. 2009. "Character Strengths: Research and Practice." *Journal of College and Character* 10 (4). https://www.tandfonline.com/doi/abs/10.2202/1940-1639.1042.

Part 2. Finding the Flow of Your Life

Activity 8. What Motivates You?

DiDomenico, S. I., and R. M. Ryan. 2017. "The Emerging Neuroscience of Intrinsic Motivation: A New Frontier in Self-Determination Research." *Frontiers in Human Neuroscience* 11: 145.

Activity 9. Getting in the Flow

Csikszentmihalyi, M. 1997. *Finding Flow: The Psychology of Engagement with Everyday Life*. New York: Basic Books.

Activity 10. Engage with Your Signature Strengths

Gander, F., R. T. Proyer, W. Ruch, and T. Wyss. 2013. "Strength-Based Positive Interventions: Further Evidence for Their Potential in Enhancing Well-Being and Alleviating Depression." *Journal of Happiness Studies* 14 (4): 1241–59.

Activity 11. Commit Random Acts of Kindness

Layous, K., S. K. Nelson, E. Oberle, K. A. Schonert-Reichl, and S. Lyubomirsky. 2012. "Kindness Counts: Prompting Prosocial Behavior in Preadolescents Boosts Peer Acceptance and Well-Being." *PLoS ONE* 7 (12): e51380.

Activity 12. Use Your Strengths to Engage Your Mind and Heart

Haridas, S., N. Bhullar, and D. A. Dunstan. 2017. "What's in Character Strengths? Profiling Strengths of the Heart and Mind in a Community Sample." *Personality and Individual Differences* 113: 32–37.

Activity 13. Overcoming Boredom

Langer, E. 1989. *Mindfulness*. Reading, MA: Addison-Wesley.

Part 3. Developing a Drama-Free (and Happy) Tribe

Activity 14. Next-Level Bully Management

Burke, J. 2016. "Posttraumatic Growth: Examining an Increase of Optimism Amongst Targets of Bullying in Ireland." *The Irish Journal of Counselling and Psychotherapy* 16: 11–15.

Activity 15. Are You My Friend or Frenemy?

Proctor, C., E. Tsukayama, A. M. Wood, J. Maltby, J. Fox Eades, and P. A. Linley. 2011. "Strengths Gym: The Impact of a Character Strengths-Based Intervention on the Life Satisfaction and Well-Being of Adolescents." *Journal of Positive Psychology* 6 (5): 377–88.

Activity 16. Your Key Relationship Strengths

Wagner, L. 2018. "Good Character Is What We Look for in a Friend: Character Strengths Are Positively Related to Peer Acceptance and Friendship Quality in Early Adolescents." *Journal of Early Adolescence* 39 (6): 864–903.

Activity 17. Stop Comparing Yourself to Others!

Festinger, L. 1954. "A Theory of Social Comparison Processes." *Human Relations* 7: 117–40.

Activity 18. Getting Off (or On) the Social Media Bandwagon

Royal Society for Public Health. Vision Voice and Practice. n.d. "Resources." https://www.rsph.org.uk/our-work/campaigns/scroll-free-september/resources.html.

Activity 19. Combatting Loneliness and Isolation

Asatryan, K. 2016. *Stop Being Lonely: Three Simple Steps to Developing Close Friendships and Deep Relationships.* Novato, CA: New World Library.

Rubin, G. 2017. "Seven Types of Loneliness (and Why It Matters)." *Gretchen Rubin* (blog). February 23. https://gretchenrubin.com/2017/02/7-types-of-loneliness.

Part 4. Cultivating What Matters Most

Activity 20. Savor Special Moments with Family

Bryant, F. B., C. M. Smart, and S. P. King. 2005. "Using the Past to Enhance the Present: Boosting Happiness Through Positive Reminiscence." *Journal of Happiness Studies* 6: 227–60.

Activity 21. Build an Attitude of Gratitude

Froh, J., and G. Bono. 2014. *Making Grateful Kids: The Science of Building Character.* West Conshohocken, PA: Templeton Press.

Activity 22. Create Mindfulness Moments of Strength

Niemiec, R. M. 2014. *Mindfulness and Character Strengths: A Practical Guide to Flourishing.* Boston: Hogrefe.

Activity 23. Mindful Walking in Nature

Diessner, R., D. Woodward, S. Stacy, and S. Mobasher. 2015. "Ten Once-a-Week Brief Beauty Walks Increase Appreciation of Natural Beauty." *Ecopsychology* 7 (3): 126–33.

Activity 24. Awe and Elevation

Algoe, S. B., and J. Haidt. 2009. "Witnessing Excellence in Action: The 'Other-Praising' Emotions of Elevation, Gratitude, and Admiration." *Journal of Positive Psychology* 4 (2): 105–27.

Activity 25. Cultivating Spirituality and the Sacred

Lipka, M., and C. Gecewicz. 2017. "More Americans Now Say That They Are Spiritual but Not Religious." *Fact Tank.* September 6. https://www.pewresearch.org/.

Pargament, K. I., A. Mahoney, J. J. Exline, J. Jones, and E. Shafranske. 2013. "Envisioning an Integrative Paradigm for the Psychology of Religion and Spirituality." In *Context, Theory, and Research,* edited by K. I. Pargament, J. Exline, and J. Jones. Vol. 1 of *APA Handbook of Psychology, Religion, and Spirituality.* Washington, DC: American Psychological Association.

Activity 26. Overcoming Jealousy, Envy, and FOMO

Muise, A., E. Christofides, and S. Desmarais. 2009. "More Information Than You Ever Wanted: Does Facebook Bring Out the Green-Eyed Monster of Jealousy?" *CyberPsychology and Behaviour* 12 (4): 441–44.

Part 5. Your Goals, Your Life

Activity 27. Your Best Possible Self

Loveday, P. M., G. P. Lovell, and C. M. Jones. 2018. "The Best Possible Selves Intervention: A Review of the Literature to Evaluate Efficacy and Guide Future Research." *Journal of Happiness Studies* 19 (2): 607–28.

Activity 28. Hope for Your Goals

Snyder, C. R., K. L. Rand, and D. R. Sigmon. 2002. "Hope Theory: A Member of the Positive Psychology Family." In *Handbook of Positive Psychology,* edited by C. R. Snyder and S. J. Lopez. New York: Oxford University Press.

Activity 29. Taming Your Inner Critic

Hutcherson, C. A., E. M. Seppala, and J. J. Gross. 2008. "Loving-Kindness Meditation Increases Social Connectedness." *Emotion* 8 (5): 720–24.

Part 6. Healthy Body, Healthy Mind

Activity 30. Promoting Good Health

Niemiec, R. M. 2019. *The Strengths-Based Workbook for Stress Relief.* Oakland, CA: New Harbinger Publications.

Goali Saedi Bocci, PhD, is an award-winning licensed clinical psychologist in private practice, published author, millennial expert, TEDx speaker, and media personality. She earned a PhD in clinical psychology from the University of Notre Dame; and completed her internship at the University of California, Berkeley, where she had the distinction of receiving a national honor when selected for the Outstanding Graduate Student/Intern Award from the American Psychological Association's Division 17. She completed her postdoctoral fellowship at Stanford University.

Saedi Bocci is a columnist for *Psychology Today*; her *Millennial Media* blog has garnered over three million hits worldwide. She is also author of *The Millennial Mental Health Toolbox, The Social Media Workbook for Teens, Digital Detox Card Deck*, and *PhDiva*. She is a highly sought-after expert for top media outlets, including *The New York Times, Newsweek, TIME*, and *ABCNews*; and has served as a recurring guest on the acclaimed morning television show, *AM Northwest*, as well as *Good Morning San Diego*. She currently serves as adjunct professor in Pepperdine University's graduate school of education and psychology. Her highest strengths are honesty, perspective, perseverance, social intelligence, hope, and zest.

Ryan M. Niemiec, PsyD, is a leading figure in the global education, research, and practice of character strengths that are found in all human beings. He is education director of the renown VIA Institute on Character, a nonprofit organization in Cincinnati, OH, that leads the advancement of the science of character strengths. He is an award-winning psychologist; certified coach; annual instructor at the University of Pennsylvania; and author and coauthor of ten books, nearly one hundred academic papers, and several-hundred user-friendly articles.

Niemiec's books include the best-selling *The Power of Character Strengths*; and other leading books, including *The Strengths-Based Workbook for Stress Relief, Character Strengths Interventions*, and *Mindfulness and Character Strengths*. As a frequent keynote speaker and workshop leader, he has offered several hundred presentations on positive psychology topics across the globe. He is a fellow of the International Positive Psychology Association, and serves on their Council of Advisors. He lives in Cincinnati, OH, with his wife and three young, zestful children. His highest strengths are hope, love, honesty, fairness, spirituality, and appreciation of beauty.

More ⏱ Instant Help Books for Teens

An Imprint of New Harbinger Publications

PUT YOUR WORRIES HERE

A Creative Journal for Teens
with Anxiety

978-1684032143 / US $17.95

THE MINDFUL TEEN

Powerful Skills to Help You Handle
Stress One Moment at a Time

978-1626250802 / US $17.95

**THE SOCIAL MEDIA
WORKBOOK FOR TEENS**

Skills to Help You Balance
Screen Time, Manage Stress &
Take Charge of Your Life

978-1684031900 / US $16.95

**THE SELF-COMPASSION
WORKBOOK FOR TEENS**

Mindfulness & Compassion Skills
to Overcome Self-Criticism &
Embrace Who You Are

978-1626259843 / US $17.95

STUFF THAT SUCKS

A Teen's Guide to Accepting
What You Can't Change &
Committing to What You Can

978-1626258655 / US $14.95

**THE TEEN GIRL'S
SURVIVAL GUIDE**

Ten Tips for Making Friends,
Avoiding Drama & Coping
with Social Stress

978-1626253063 / US $17.95

🌱 new harbinger publications

1-800-748-6273 / newharbinger.com

(VISA, MC, AMEX / prices subject to change without notice)
Follow Us 📷 📘 🐦 ▶ 📌 💼